How To
Build a
Pro Streetbike

How To
Build a
Pro Streetbike

Mike Seate

with photos by Simon Green, Scott O'Dell, David Avila,

Miles Davis, Kim Love, Joe Appel, and Shawn Stinett

MOTORBOOKS

First published in 2006 by Motorbooks, an imprint of MBI Publishing Company, Galtier Plaza, Suite 200, 380 Jackson Street, St. Paul, MN 55101-3885 USA

MBI Publishing Company titles are also available at discounts in bulk quantity for industrial or sales-promotional use. For details write to Special Sales Manager at MBI Publishing Company, Galtier Plaza, Suite 200, 380 Jackson Street, St. Paul, MN 55101-3885 USA

Editor: Peter Schletty
Designer: Chris Fayers

Printed in China

Library of Congress Cataloging-in-Publication Data

Seate, Mike.
 How to build a pro streetbike / Mike Seate.
    p. cm.
  ISBN-13: 978-0-7603-2450-9 (softbound)
  ISBN-10: 0-7603-2450-6 (softbound)
 1. Motorcycles--Customizing. 2. Home-built motorcycles. I. Title.
TL440S388 2007
 629.28'775--dc22

                              2006024562

Mike Seate is a newspaper columnist for the Pittsburgh Tribune-Review *and a producer for TV's Speed Channel. He has written several books on motorcycling, and is an avid rider who can usually be seen at track days or riding the backroads near his home in western Pennsylvania.*

On the cover: Main: New York's Dennis Pagalilauan inspired Yamaha with his tasteful 2000 R-1 street and show machine. *Photo by Joe Appel* Inset: The feed tube from a nitrous bottle is fed to the Hayabusa's bank of fuel injectors.

On the title page: Genuine track-only rides like this Kawasaki ZX-6R from the California Superbike School are stripped of all lighting equipment, street plastic, and passenger accommodation.

On the back cover: This Suzuki Bandit streetfighter received a swingarm from a Honda VFR 750, which bolts on easily to the stock frame mounts.

CONTENTS

FOREWORD: Custom Sportbikes– The New Choppers

Thanks to near-saturation coverage on television, anchored by "reality stars" like Billy Lane and Orange County Choppers' Teutel family, *chopper* is now a household word. But as a result of all this overexposure, choppers have lately lost their luster among serious custom motorcycle enthusiasts who covet the power, speed, and badass style these hand-built motorcycles once symbolized. Today's choppers have become a ridiculous parody of themselves. Too many gaudy theme bikes with beer-can-shaped gas tanks or golf-ball-styled wheel covers, not to mention the "boutique biker" culture that has every investment banker slapping on chaps and a clip-on ponytail for his Sunday morning ride around the block on some $50K cookie-cutter kit bike. Modern choppers are left with all the outlaw attitude of a set of designer cufflinks.

All of this brings us around to the subject of the book at hand—custom sportbikes. While we watch choppers devolve into a clumsy caricature of what once made them great, the custom sportbike scene is poppin' with freshness. From Detroit to Daytona Beach, from Brooklyn to the Bay Area, the streets are ruled by tight superbikes that put yesterday's Evo-powered billet barges to shame. A new breed of custom sportbike tuners and builders—young, aggressive, and unapologetically performance-driven—have stood up to fill in the gap and create a new style of custom motorcycle, utterly badass custom sportbikes that are ripped with attitude, like menacing middle-fingers on wheels.

The most appealing aspect of the custom sportbike culture is that there are no rules. In the chopper realm there is essentially one bike that you are allowed to build: the same big-bore V-twin engine slotted into the same stretched frame. The only things separating one from another are the brand of billet bits bolted on and the hue of candy paint sprayed over the top. Custom sportbikes, on the other hand, are all over the map: Drag-race-derived GSX-Rs with stretched swingarms and nitrous bottles, MotoGP-inspired Ducatis decked out with a crateload of carbon fiber, punked-up Bandit streetfighters, even stunted out CBRs with 12-bars and chromed-out crash cages are all cool, and all show loads more class than the same-old Fat Boy tail-dragger. Tricked out sportbikes are the next movement.

This is what makes this burgeoning custom sportbike scene such an exciting, vibrant, and vital place to be. The whole impetus of building a custom motorcycle is to have something utterly unique and individualized, a two-wheeled, 200-mile per hour expression of your own personality. The motivation for customizing your motorcycle is typically to create something unique and original, unlike anyone else's ride, so you stand out at the local bike night or wherever else you ride. And the intention of this book is to help you do just that.

The art of custom sportbikes has grown by leaps and bounds in the past few years, progressing from basic bolt-on mods to daring one-off fabrication and innovation that is equal to (or beyond) anything ever seen in the chopper world. "Dare to be different" is the custom bike builder's credo, and it's also the aim of this book—to give you the motivation, ideas and, most importantly, the hands-on skills to create a kick-ass custom sportbike all your own. Your vision of the perfect custom might be a stripped-down, high-handlebar streetfighter; a polished-and-plated show bike; or a nasty, stretched and slammed, 400-horsepower turbocharged drag strip refugee. Regardless of the details, the chapters of this book will give you the ideas, resources, and the mechanical know-how to get you started down the custom sportbike path.

Though the projects in this book vary from mild to wild, they all have two elements in common: an unapologetic pursuit of speed and performance, and an undeniably aggressive attitude. These are traits inherent in sportbikes and the sportbike culture, and essential to the sportbike experience. These are the traits that set custom sportbikes apart from yesterday's custom motorcycles, and that cement the sportbike's position as the dominant custom bike of the future. Don't look back. Get involved in this new custom motorcycle movement, and do your part to push custom sportbike design into new and uncharted directions. Read this book, pick up your wrench and welding torch, and get started on your own version of tomorrow's sickest custom bike today.

—Aaron Frank
Editor-in-Chief
Super Streetbike magazine

INTRODUCTION

On the surface, there's not much that needs improving on a modern sportbike. The mainstream manufacturers have been studying what backstreet builders have been doing with their product for long enough that customers can basically walk into any motorcycle dealership and ride out on a machine that looks like it was designed by a one-man shop, not a corporate committee. Just a decade ago, streetfighter-style motorcycles were the sole property of a handful of speed- and style-crazed urban riders on the avenues of Europe. These stripped-down, Mad Max machines are now offered—albeit in a slightly more civilized form—by every firm from Aprilia and Triumph to Buell and Kawasaki.

A quarter-century ago, performance-minded street riders with racing aspirations got busy building their own fully faired roadracers in home paddocks and trackside garages. Today, the current generation of supersport motorcycles could easily whip butt on any 25-year-old Grand Prix machine out of the box, without turning a single bolt.

There are bolt-on turbocharging systems galore, easy-to-install nitrous hook-up kits, and big bore engine parts to turn a weekday commuter into a true, drag strip screamer. We're offered endless choices of color schemes and flashy graphics, and most manufacturers work in conjunction with the big aftermarket performance houses to ensure that horsepower hop-up kits hit the showrooms at the same time as this year's must-have 190-mile per hour missiles.

In a climate like this, one would think the need to spend weeks or months and a knee-high stack of C-notes to take torch, hacksaw, and wrench to a sportbike would have become a quaint memory. But as a visit to any superbike race, drag strip, or motorcycle stunt show will reveal, the sportbike arms race taking place in the showrooms has only spurred custom builders to become more competitive. If they offer us 180 horsepower and a 10-second quarter-mile, it's only a matter of hours before some ballsy throttle jockey starts wondering, "OK, but how about a nine-second E.T. and 220 horses?"

Chromed, stretched, and flamed, this street-or-strip Yamaha YZFR-1 is as pretty as it is fast.

And that's all good as far as we're concerned. The emergence of the tuner-bike generation, the popularity of slammed and lowered street draggers, tail-scraping stunt-bikes, and pieces of rolling art capable of terminal speeds that would shame a light aircraft—these are a natural reaction to the Original Equipment Manufacturers' (OEM) attempts to market what their sales committees think we want. A similar need to one-up the big boys helped fuel the chopper rebirth that's forever changed the face of cruiser motorcycles.

And like the chopper movement, where builders often abandon any pretense of ergonomic comfort, precise handling and everyday usability in a search for the perfect aesthetic, tuner-bike builders are also pushing the limits of form over function. Sure, an 8-inch-wide rear rim with a 300-millimeter tire isn't going to cause your machine to handle like an AMA Supersport bike. And dropping your forks 3 inches, extending the swingarm a half-foot, and removing an "unnecessary" second from the brake rotor isn't going to do much for your sport-touring excursions. But damned if these—and a million other mods—don't make a generation of already stylish and impressive motorcycles even more exciting, more unique, and most of all, more "ours."

So as the showrooms fill up with factory fighters and supersport machines designed by CAD systems and demographic surveys, you can bet your pink slip there will be rid-ers, racers, stunters, and builders searching for a way to outdo them.

While it's common to see all of these types of machines parked together at a motorcycle gathering, not many riders have the time, interest, or resources to build or ride more than just one. Each separate type of custom sportbike brings with it the need to purchase unique (read: expensive) parts and accessories. And the technical requirements needed to build a wide-tire GSX-R, for instance, are a lot more demanding than those needed to prep your ride for a weekend of circle wheelies.

With that in mind, we designed this book to provide a complete chronicle of a ground-up building project for five very different types of sportbike. This way, a reader whose tastes may change over time has a resource guide at hand that can come in handy when they want to, say, give up trips down the local quarter-mile for Run What You Brung Night and instead try their hand at stunting or track days. We've also searched our archives to present some of the wildest, hairiest, and most insane custom sportbikes on the planet, culled from visits to race paddocks, streets, strips, and parking lots in places as exotic as the Isle of Man and the MotoGP races at Laguna Seca. We hope their presence inspires your next custom sportbike project to be one that turns heads, runs quick, and silences the competition.

Fast and beautiful, Bimota's Italian sportbikes respond well to custom paint and other cosmetic modifications. This one even fared well in a public road race held in Pittsburgh's Schenley Park.

CHAPTER 1
A SLAMMED AND LOWERED 'BUSA: THE UNDISPUTED KING OF PRO STREETBIKES

Ask some tuner bike enthusiasts why Suzuki's GSX1300R Hayabusa is the most popular customized sportbike, and the answers you'll hear are as different as the ways this big mutha of a roadster is altered. Some say the 'Busa has caught on with urban riders, street and strip drag racers, and bling merchants because of its voluptuous bodywork. Designed in-house by Suzuki Motor Corporation way back in 1998, the Hayabusa's skin has remained so popular with sportbike fans that it's the only model in the Hamamatsu firm's lineup that remains unchanged to this day.

Others herald the big four-banger because it arrived on the streets with 170 rear-wheel horsepower and the uniquely lawyer-inducing ability to reach a top speed of nearly 198 miles per hour in stock form. Add an aftermarket exhaust and a freer-breathing airbox, and the magic 200-mile per hour mark was fast approaching on any Hayabusa rider's horizon. For a nation of motorcycling speed freaks raised on other top-speed missiles like Kawasaki's Z-1s of the 1970s and Kawasaki's GPZ series of a decade later, the chance to own a bike that could outrun most light aircraft was too much to resist.

On the mean streets of the Dirty South, where elapsed times always meant more to sportbikers than cornering clearance, second- and third-generation street racers embraced the idea of a motorbike that looked like some kind of weird bird (it was named in honor of Japan's fastest birds of prey) but had enough comfort to take the lady along for a ride, and enough throw-down to hook up at a stoplight and burn an eighth-mile in six seconds. It had all the right elements: A large-capacity, easily tuneable, four-cylinder Japanese motor, a burgeoning aftermarket to support even the craziest whims of a home tuner, and acceleration that felt like nothing that had come before.

That tuners and high-performance engine builders also took to the Hayabusa should have come as no surprise to

Custom Sportbike Concepts went the patriotic route with this red, white, and blue 'Busa street dragger.

A Hotbodies Racing undertail cleans up the rear end of this Yamaha R-1 while hiding the underseat exhausts nicely.

Unbolting one of the front brake calipers and discarding the disc is an old drag racer's trick popularized by street riders.

anyone. The manufacturer deliberately retarded the motorcycle's performance capabilities to just under the magic 200-mile per hour mark. To many, this was a smart way to avoid offending safety regulators on the lookout for vehicles to keep from public roads. To a man like Tim Brown, it was an open provocation, a challenge to see just how thinly the cylinder walls could be rebored, how much turbo boost the engine cases could withstand before spewing their guts, and just how ballsy a rider needed to be to handle such a machine. As a result, the Suzuki Hayabusa has become the focus point of one of the fastest-growing custom motorcycle movements in the world.

"When that bike came out, there was absolutely no question that it was top dawg. So everybody who thought they were fast, or was fast, wanted one," said Nick Anglada, owner of Custom Sportbike Concepts in Wintergarden, Florida. "Right away, that meant the aftermarket companies had to come up with custom and performance parts, even before the bikes were in the showrooms."

Anglada said Suzukis have always been popular motorcycles for customizing because many of their parts are interchangeable with those from other Suzuki sportbikes. "If you know what you're doing, you can take the stronger swingarm from, say, a GSX-R 1000 and bolt it onto a 'Busa, or use the radial brake caliper mounts from a GSX-R on a 'Busa and it will stop like it's hit a brick wall. You break something, you go down to a junkyard and use the parts off another Suzuki sportbike. They can be incredibly cheap to run. It's the Escalade of sportbikes because there are just tons of accessories," said Anglada, who tricked out his first 'Busa in 1998.

It's not unusual to see Hayabusas outfitted with velocity enhancements, including nitrous oxide canisters that can provide instant boost to the tune of 100 extra horses, and elaborate turbochargers that can add repeated boosts upward of 250 horsepower at the rear wheel. The aftermarket has also responded to this bike with literally tons of individual custom parts, more than any other Japanese motorcycle. This means a Hayabusa has the ability to look as good as it is fast.

Rick's Motorcycles of Plaistow, New Hampshire, turned this ordinary Honda CBR 900RR into a show-winner, using parts from other Hondas and lots of gold plating.

Want a 'Busa with all-carbon fiber bodywork designed to slip through the air like Superman with an oily complexion problem? No sweat. Want to make your 'Busa lower, lighter, and longer for more efficient launches? Want a lock-up clutch, air-shifter, recessed neon lighting, day-glow logos carved into your paintwork, or a rear-view camera so you don't have to spoil your 1300's wind-tunnel-tested aerodynamics with mirrors? Aftermarket cams, preported heads, forged pistons, and drop-in big bore kits? The Hayabusa rider has access to all of these stylistic and performance enhancements and more.

For our project bike, we enlisted the help of Rick's Motorcycles, a New Hampshire tuner bike shop that's turned out some of the slickest, sickest Hayabusas we've seen. With so many custom and tuning options available to the 'Busa owner, the guys at Rick's decided to hook

Right: The business end of a whopping 300-millimeter rear tire on Rick's custom CBR—fun to look at, less fun to clean!

Above: Build a stunner like this lizard-scaled Hayabusa, and you can't keep the crowds away!

Right: Notice the amazing gas tank detail on Jose Rodriguez's Hayabusa that won the 2005 Palm Beach Custom Sportbike Build-Off. The seat is genuine alligator skin!

Left: You don't want to brake too hard on this bike. Check out the chromed, spiked hardware around the cockpit and topping the fork tubes.

Below: A tasteful two-tone paint scheme, lowered suspension, and a custom matched seat make this mildly customized Hayabusa a standout.

Right: A bike like this will pay for itself at the quarter-mile and draw crowds daily.

Below: Hahn Racing lowering links drop this 'Busa's rear suspension 3 inches though a small amount of travel remains for cornering.

their chosen ride up with a few of the more popular and difficult-to-master modifications on the market.

An extended swingarm was selected, as this is one of the first mods most performance-minded 'Busa owners opt for. By lengthening the bike's already considerable 59-inch wheelbase, the machine is far less likely to wheelie during a rapid launch. Likewise, many drag racing Hayabusa tuners drop the machine's front forks a couple of inches in the triple clamps or opt to install a complete internal lowering kit. These shortened versions of the stock fork springs not only look the business, but when coupled with a set of lowering links (or a shortened shock absorber, which is a far more costly option) at the rear, it's another step toward making the bike launch hard and straight with as little oscillation as possible—just like the pro street dragsters.

From there, the crew at Rick's decided to add a twin turbocharger handcrafted by motorcycle drag racing legend Barry Henson of Velocity Racing. Aftermarket cams from tuning experts Yoshimura and, if your heart can stand it, a nitrous oxide system. While some would characterize equipping a motorcycle already capable of 190 miles per hour with an additional 100 or so horses a bit of overkill, Hayabusa pilots know there's no such concept. "We wanted to take a near-stock bike and add all the sorts of things that would make for a really pimped-out, crazy-fast streetbike that can even surprise people at the drag strip," said Rick's chief mechanic B.J. Basnett.

He and his brother John, the shop's co-owner, were determined to create one of the sickest 'Busas on the road. Their clever custom touches include a 300-series rear tire

Jimmy Brown of Myrtle Beach, South Carolina, built this NASCAR-themed pro street Suzuki for a customer. I wonder what it will do at Daytona?

Slamming and lowering your streetbike doesn't have to sacrifice its functionality. This 1990 Suzuki GSX-R 1100 is raced, stunted, and ridden long distances.

on a pair of Performance Machine rims and some tasty Arlen Ness chopper parts, including the chromed footpegs and billet aluminum rear view mirrors. "When we build a custom out of a bike like this, we want to show people there's really no limit to what you can do with your motorcycle," John said. How true.

ORIGINAL PHATSTER

The battle over which custom builder created the very first 300-series rear end for a Hayabusa is an argument as fervently contested as the one over who made the first chopper a few decades ago.

Down in Myrtle Beach, South Carolina, sportbike builder Eric Shahan's claims to the phat-type throne are among the most respected, Shahan having busted out on the streets with *Money Shot*, this ultimate bling machine back in 2004. Shahan's motorcycle is memorable for its bubble-butt rear end and for the clever, imaginative detailing, unlike anything else on the market.

The finish is a wild combination of Imron paint in multicolored tribal murals and life-sized copies of $100 bills printed on vinyl and pasted directly to the Hayabusa's bodywork. The finish was far from easy to apply, the builder says, with the delicate vinyl stickers requiring intricate cutting in among the painted parts.

While his in-house painter tackled the details of finishing the bodywork, Shahan's shop, 360 Motorsports, tackled the shine factor, chroming the frame, adding a set of

Shahan's 360 Motorsports builds each of its extended, wide swingarms from aircraft-grade billet aluminum, including a jackshaft to run the twin drive chains.

Eric Shahan, rolling large on his custom 'Busa.

Performance Machine wheels and stretched swingarm, while the mechanical experts at 360 set to work on the very unusual rear end. A close look reveals there to be two, not one, drive chains powering the 300-millimeter rear rim, a feat possible only through the deployment of a set of custom-made twin jackshafts. The stock drive chain powers the second sprocket located just inside the thick, billet aluminum swingarm, made with 3-inch-thick sidewalls dense enough to handle such a beefy rear tire.

Shahan swears the bike still handles as smoothly as it did with the stock 190-millimeter rear tire in place, though we've heard other wide-tire proponents confess that tilting one of these long, low, and wide runners into a sharp turn requires some seriously big cajones. But apparently Shahan has that area covered as well—you'll notice a pair of big green ones hanging from the swingarm!

The open megaphone exhaust has no internal baffling, which is great for the drag strip and even better for annoying the neighbors. The engine has stock displacement, the only additions being a Lockhart Phillips ignition advancer, K&N air filters, and a Barnett clutch kit needed to keep the plats from burning up when *Money Shot* smokes the rear tire.

Phat is where it's at for pro street riders, perfectly illustrated by this 12-inch wide rear rubber.

NIGHTMARE ON YOUR STREET

Tim Brown's Alum-A-Chrome is probably the best-known custom shop in the tuner empire, having built motorcycles for high-profile customers. Their clientele includes rappers, NBA stars, and the odd street riders with the bucks to turn one of Brown's high-concept machines into reality. With over 15 years in the business, Brown says he's actually watched the streetbike scene contract a little in recent years, as many of the big ballers who first helped launch his business have had to back off of the more outlandish custom projects.

"There was a time when the sky really was the limit. Guys would walk in here with paper bags full of $50s and $100s, telling me a basic idea and coming back after I'd had license to build whatever I could dream up. Now a lot of those guys have wives, kids, and mortgages, so you don't see the really big-dollar projects as often," said Brown, who's work has landed him on national TV shows including Speed Channel's *2 Wheel Tuesday* with Greg White.

Though Brown's main cheddar these days is derived from an extensive chrome parts exchange business—which maintains a thoroughly cataloged stock of over 5,000 replacement parts for most sportbikes—he still hears the occasional call to blow minds with an over-the-top bling machine. Back in 2001, he busted out with his first Hayabusa based on the popular horror movie villain Freddie Krueger of *Nightmare on Elm Street*. The bike made

continued on page 21

the
Money
$hot

Above: The LCD screen molded into the rear seat hump plays horror flicks in Tim Brown's Nightmare On Your Street showbike.

Left: This Alum-A-Chrome bike features a cut-and-raked frame and a Legends air-ride rear suspension unit for a pavement-scraping ride.

Opposite: The paint scheme on Money Shot includes color copies of real $100 bills made of vinyl. Neat effect, but not advised by the U.S. Secret Service!

Right: A Hahn Racing turbo exits from the mouth of the clever, molded-in hockey mask, while the mural on the fairings took over a month to complete. Building a show-winner takes patience.

Below: Aftermarket bodywork abounds for the at-home 'Busa builder, offering advanced aerodynamics and sleeker lines.

John Dantzler of Two Wheel Customs in Charlotte, North Carolina, is considered by many to be a genius in the slammed bike trade.

The plastic bodywork on this 'Busa was initially copper-plated to help the chrome adhere to the parts.

continued from page 17

waves for its combination of wicked, one-off parts, a funky paint scheme incorporating a snarling Krueger and bloody slash marks throughout, and copious amounts of chrome. Brown tore that machine down a few years later after receiving a challenge to enter a custom sportbike contest sponsored by *Super Streetbike* magazine. Like Krueger himself, Brown's most famous 'Busa seems to have 1,000 lives and different incarnations.

For the rebuilt version, Brown's crew again took the Suzuki down to a bare frame, rechroming the entire frame, forks, and engine covers before really hyping things up. Inside the hand-molded fairings is a Mr. Turbo system boosting the already bored-out motor to near 330 rear-wheel horsepower.

With an eye for the dramatic, Brown ensured that the turbo's exhaust fumes would exit through a horror-movie

With everything dipped in the shiny stuff, these custom Suzukis weigh a good 60 pounds more than a stock bike.

hockey mask molded into the left side lower fairing. The bodywork was extensively customized from front to back, the huge passenger seat hump now home to a 7-inch LCD screen playing slasher flicks, naturally.

At the rear, a single-sided swingarm grabs hold of a 300-millimeter rear tire, the wheels, and a set of dazzling spinner rims from Florida's Custom Sportbike Concepts featuring arrowhead-shaped tines.

When viewed in the metal, Brown's machine has an almost freakishly long wheelbase, a look he achieved by adding a Legends air glide lowering system to the bike while cutting and raking the front end an additional eight degrees over stock.

This is perhaps the first time we've seen this done to a sportbike, and the effects are mind-blowing. Additional touches include an ostrich skin seat cover, full LED lighting, and murals painted along the upper frame section. While some would say the real nightmare in a bike like this is the $50,000 price tag, you have to agree it would certainly scare away the competition.

Dantzler painted the chromed nose fairing with dark candy green paint, adding matching light covers for a cohesive effect.

Right: Though adding a single-sided swingarm conversion to a custom slammed bike can add over $5,000 to construction costs, it is a sharp function accessory.

Below: This Hayabusa contains the perfect blend of dazzling paint and just enough chrome.

HEAVY D

North Carolina's John Dantzler is the builder with perhaps the most confidence in the performance capabilities of Suzuki's largest displacement sportbike. Dantzler, who runs Charlotte's Two Wheel Customs, is the first builder on the national scene to have chrome plated an entire GSX1300R, a process that's proven bright enough to blind pilots in low-flying aircraft, and bold enough to create a legion of imitators.

Dantzler says dipping the plastic fairings into the vats is a far more complex process than many think. Chrome, a liquid metal, can be made to adhere to magnesium wheels, engine covers, and chassis parts rather easily. Plastic parts, such as seat units and fairings, must first be submerged in an electrostatically charged copper solution to help the chrome seize on the surface.

Two Wheel Customs began experimenting with this process soon after it became available and has survived the resultant trials and errors. "The chromed plastic parts don't bend after they're plated, so we had one hell of a time getting all the bodywork back together without breaking anything," the builder recalled.

With the chrome situation locked down, Dantzler's crew set about experimenting with ways to take the shiny stuff one step further. This Hayabusa street rod features flame decals designed by Dantzler, copied from photographs of

A SLAMMED AND LOWERED 'BUSA: THE
UNDISPUTED KING OF PRO STREETBIKES

actual flames and applied to the machine to break up the oceans of chrome.

Sitting in the saddle of this low-riding ghetto blaster revealed just how much extra weight the chrome plating added to the machine: 60 pounds! Still, the builder says the stock 180-horsepower motor is more than strong enough to handle the added heft, particularly after he tore into the water-cooled powerplant, adding a set of big bore J&E pistons, a set of Yoshimura cams, ported heads, and oversized racing valves. A hidden nitrous bottle brings the ponies over the 225 mark, good for a top speed somewhere near 210 miles per hour, Dantzler says.

Instead of just lowering the front end—a trick many street riders do by tying a set of canvas tie-down straps to the triple clamps—Dantzler spared no expense, throwing on an air ride suspension system. The machine now rocks up for street riding or squats down-and-dirty for drag strip action with a 4-inch suspension travel provided by a small on-board compressor.

An Adams superlong swingarm is on board at the rear, designed with 3 to 9 inches of adjustment. Up in the cockpit, there's plenty of evidence of the veritable candy store of custom goodies available to the Hayabusa owner: Knurled and embossed aluminum grips, a chromed top clamp embossed with the bike's logo in Japanese script, and gauges in special glow-in-the-dark colors. Variations on this chromed-to-the-hilt theme are an interesting option for at-home 'Busa builders, and Dantzler points out that part of its appeal is that riders can chrome as much or as little of their machines as they wish—interspersing the shiny stuff with painted panels, for example—and chroming other parts when funds allow

.

THE BEAST WITHIN

If breaking the rules of what can be done to a custom sportbike was Dennis Vasquez's goal when he designed the *Hayabeasta*, he more than succeeded. The owner of New Jersey's Pit Stop Motorsports built what has been called the world's most arresting custom sportbike for hip-hop videographer J.J. Smith, starting with a basically stock 2002 Suzuki and a vision of "creating a motorcycle that captured Smith's personality and work."

As the high-profile director behind videos for top-flight rappers like DMX, Wu Tang Clan, and Master P, Smith's work generally displays a surreal, dark world where motorcycles scream by on one wheel, raging pit bulls bay like gargoyles, and there's enough fire and brimstone to hide all sorts of monsters. Vasquez, who has built a stable of incredibly detailed custom sporting tackle over the past decade, sought a means of bringing this dark vision to life. The focal

Opposite: Dennis Vasquez's Hayabeasta *features a three-dimensional demon face made from a saber-toothed tiger jawbone and lots of imagination.*
Above: The wild paint scheme is matched to the helmet for a memorable effect.

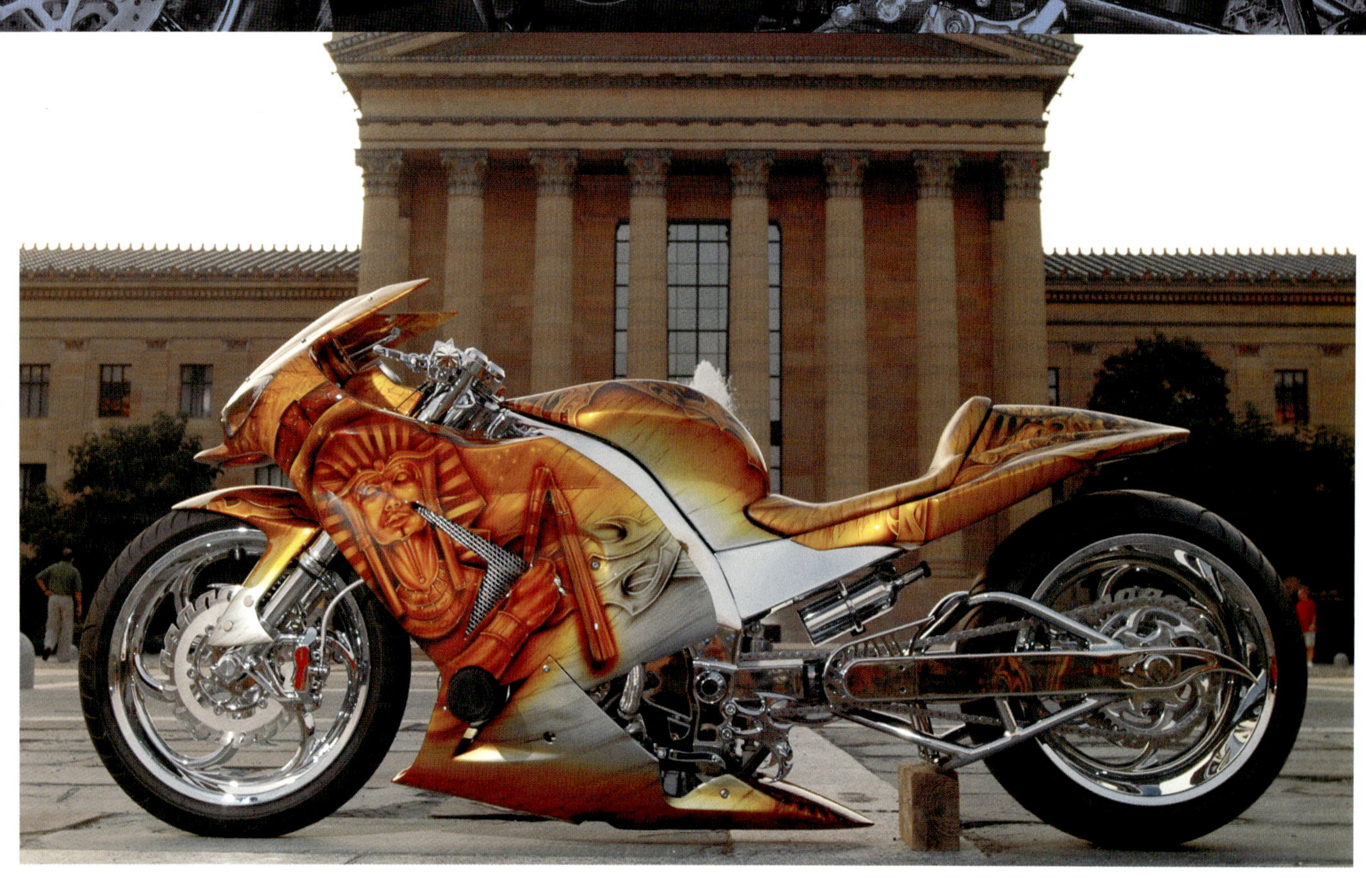

Steve Kehler of Philadelphia's Tricked Out Custom Cycles created this stunning custom from a Kawasaki ZX10R, using 100 LED lights, copious chroming, hand-machined billet aluminum fork clamps, and pieces of bodywork from several bikes including a Yamaha R-1 (tail section grafted onto fairing sides), a Suzuki Hayabusa (fairing lowers), and a Yamaha R-6 (headlights). A turbocharger and twin nitrous bottles take the Kawasaki's already formidable performance to an unheard-of 280 horsepower.

point of the machine, of course, is the mad, gaping jaw covering the front fairing.

Designing and fabricating the 3D sculpture over the original headlights of the 'Busa was an exercise in theatrical artistry; Vasquez said he used a jaw and fangs from a saber-toothed tiger skull he'd purchased at a theatrical supply store—well, that and plenty of Bondo molding putty. To further create his surreal take on a growling beast of a bike, Vasquez mounted a pair of halogen driving lights above the mouth, beaming light to the road through a pair of 3D eyes.

Instead of simply stopping there, the crew at Pit Stop invested hundreds of hours in creating a theme motorcycle with a cohesive look. That meant stripping off the remaining bodywork and shipping it off to their painters at Neso Graphics in New York. There, an intricate pattern of beastly muscles, sinews, and scales was applied in a ghostly blue, purple, and metallic black tone. Staring at the *Hayabeasta* from axle to axle, these shapes morph into naked ladies, screaming skulls and a host of other designs that have given the competition plenty of nightmares.

Like all the best show 'Busas, this machine has had its frame fully show-chromed, its stock rims replaced with a set of chromed Gatlin wheels from California's Performance Machine, and a set of wicked Galfer wave brake rotors added for control. Vasquez also created room in the under-tail for a special-construction four-into-two exhaust system from Britain's Blue Flame. Inside the beast, Vasquez kept the motor internals in a relatively mild state of tune, while other detail touches include a set of chromed and knurled handgrips from chopper builder Eddie Trotta, blue neon accent lights dispersed throughout the frame and bodywork, and one of Pit Stop's own horizontal license plate hangers. The blue tires come courtesy of Tomahawk, a British company that recently began offering multicolored rubber to American riders.

We've seen less-experienced builders create similar effects using helmets, real skulls, and military paraphernalia that's been molded into their 'Busa's bodywork, but we can't stress enough knowing full well how difficult and time consuming this sort of undertaking can be. In recent years, some aftermarket companies have even begun offering customers do-it-yourself kits of bodywork panels featuring injection-molded 3D designs for easier custom creations. Vasquez just laughs when asked how much time and money was

Matte black and already a fast pro street ride, the Rick's Motorcycles project ready for tear-down.

invested in the project, but we can assume that neither investment was minimal. The result, however, is a showbike that's bold and different enough to nearly change the custom 'Busa game in one stroke.

THE BUILD

The Rick's Motorcycles project bike started off already partially customized. Back in 2003, the previous owner equipped the new Hayabusa with a 10-inch-over CNS swingarm made from billet aluminum, chromed rims coated in a slick red candy powdercoat, and a few other go-fast accessories. The crew at Rick's, however, figured that the flat black beauty could go one step farther, and they hooked the bike up with what chief mechanic John described as "all the kinds of things you'd do to a pro streetbike if money was no object."

That involved stripping the near-stock ride down to the bare frame, a laborious process that starts with unbolting the fairings and bodywork, and disconnecting all the electrical wiring, gas lines, and fittings. John stresses the importance of labeling the disassembled parts and placing all hardware in clearly marked containers to help the rebuild move along smoothly.

A complete teardown on a bike with a few thousand miles on the engine provides an excellent opportunity to check out wear and tear on driveline components and other moving parts. As the crew removed the extended swingarm for rechroming, for instance, they replaced the bearings, doing the same on the bearings in the headstock. Though this bike will eventually roll on a Tricky suspension system, builders who choose to stay with a traditional damper shock setup might want to have the suspension rebuilt while the bike is disassembled.

The Hayabusa donor bike arrived with a fairly strong motor, a 1,400-cc big-bore kit and a set of Yoshimura drop-in cams already installed. Though the team had briefly considered adding a turbo, they figured they'd save time and expense by utilizing a bolt-on wet-nitrous kit from NOS. The unit's power cords splice into the stock wiring harness at the ECU box, which can be a fairly complex job, Rick Basnett says. It took the Rick's crew about five hours to completely wire in the NOS system, and once hooked in, they then fed the feeding tube for the nitrous nozzle into the combustion chamber. Builder B.J. Basnett says the Hayabusa's head can be easily drilled and tapped to accept

27

the NOS nozzle, which facilitates feeding the fuel and nitrous directly into the combustion chamber for better effect. This setup is far superior to what's known as a "dry" nitrous system, B.J. says, in which the gas is fed into the airbox, which allows far less of it to burn. When armed, B.J. Basnett says, the wet nitrous system will feed the gas into the throttle bodies as activated by an electronic throttle position sensor that's included in the kit.

With the powerplant sorted, the crew at Rick's focused on the drivetrain, adding a Barnett lock-up clutch that allows drag racers to launch their bikes without worrying about clutch slippage. The original bike ran a full Yoshimura four-into-one exhaust system, reputed to add about 12 rear-wheel horsepower at the top end of the rev range. This time, the 'Busa would speak to the world via a Brock Racing Sidewinder megaphone system that has less restrictive baffles and adds about 15 peak horsepower at the top end. The Brock pipe's right-side exit also helps with this motorcycle's particularly low profile—unlike a traditional system that exits from the bottom of the fairing, the Brock pipe will not scrape the pavement.

Left: The bodywork is removed and placed in safekeeping for repainting.
Below: With the wiring harness unhooked from the lights and power equipment, the crew begins preparing the engine for removal.

Above: After draining the coolant, the stock radiator's six mounting bolts are backed out for removal. Right: The 'Busa project bike's front forks are pulled so they can be chromed and shortened 2 inches.

For cosmetics, the entire frame was nickel-plated, a process that was once popular with café racer builders and is much more durable—and less difficult to clean—than chrome. The CNS swingarm was replaced by a longer billet arm, specially manufactured wide enough to accept the 12-inch rim. The front forks were also replaced by a set from a Suzuki GSX-R 1000, favored for its outstanding radial caliper mounts located on the wheel spindles. Once the triple clamps were fitted to the Hayabusa chassis to make sure all the new front end components fit properly, the unit was torn down and sent off to the chromer. Internally, the GSX-R 1000 fork springs were cut down by about 2 inches, which lends the machine a slammed, drag strip look and helps for more controlled high-rpm launches.

Wildest of all, the Rick's crew engineered this bike to run without use of a traditional sidestand, facilitating the use of an elaborate lowering system. Based around an electronically activated air ride suspension system, the motorcycle's rear end can be raised or lowered thanks to a small on-board compressor hidden beneath the rear passenger seat hump.

NOS
The Leader in Nitrous Technology!

Opposite top: Back from the chromer's shop, the crew begin the painstaking rebuild process.

Opposite bottom left: Christmas arrives early. A Nitrous Express kit will be added, boosting horsepower to the 200 range.

Opposite bottom right: Nitrous kits require careful installation, and this one is no exception.

Above: Custom rearset footpegs have been chromed to match the engine covers and frame.

Right: The feed tube from the nitrous bottle is fed to the Hayabusa's bank of fuel injectors.

The airbox, now equipped with a free-breathing K&N filter, is reattached above the fuel injectors.

Instead of utilizing a sidestand, the bike can be lowered directly on to the bellypan, possible after the crew cut a section of the lower fairing away. They then welded a 2-inch flat aluminum skid plate to the bottom of the oil pan while the engine sat on the workbench, allowing the bike to be lowered onto its motor without damaging any essential parts.

The Air Ride system runs about $950 and can be spliced into the motorcycle's stock wiring harness fairly easily. The system draws a minimal amount of power from the battery and can even be activated by a small, handheld remote. On the street, the guys at Rick's swear the Air Ride system offers a good 3 inches of travel, which makes the 'Busa ride no different than most slammed and lowered pro street machines.

The crew encountered the most challenging work when it came to mounting the 300-series Avon rear tire. The wheel is constructed from a pair of GSX-R 1000 rims, split open and welded together with about 5 inches of additional material installed in the center. The extreme width of the rim means mounting tires can be a genuine headache, but the look of the fat rim—along with the fact that it's almost wide enough to allow the bike to be parked without a kick-stand—says it all. Extra care was used to ensure that at least ½ inch of space was left surrounding the rear tire, as the rubber will expand when in use. Though many firms, including Custom Sportbike Concepts, manufacture wide tire swingarms in traditional and single-sided varieties, experienced builders can cut existing arms and weld in additional material to save on costs.

With the rear end sorted, the crew set about customizing the Hayabusa's bodywork. This consisted mostly of plastic welding additional material over the stock headlight, taillight, and turn signal holes, then cutting out the desired shapes in the new plastic. This is relatively easy with an electric Dremel tool or bodyman's knife, though it's important to attach some kind of insulation to the back side of the bodywork around the headlight to avoid burn-in on the light visor. The engine cases, clutch cover, and other hard parts were all chromed, and the guys at Rick's said they made sure to test-tap any threaded holes on these parts before refitting them to make sure there was no plating clogging the access.

Painted and rewired, the machine was then ready to hit the streets.

Above: The rear tire is test-mounted in place on the new swingarm. Note the importance of balancing the front end to avoid any workshop accidents. Right: Made from two 6-inch rims bolted together, with additional material TIG-welded in the center, the new wheel measures 12 inches between the sidewalls.

RESOURCE GUIDE

Rick's Motorcycles
Plastic repair, bike fabrication
(800) 423-1320
ricksmotorcycles.com

Brock's Performance Products
Exhaust systems
(937) 298-6818
brocksperformance.com

Roaring Toyz
Extended swingarms, custom Hayabusa products
(941) 953-4423
roaringtoyz.com

RPM Cycle Performance
Hayabusa specialists
(870) 863-4630
rpmcycleperformance.com

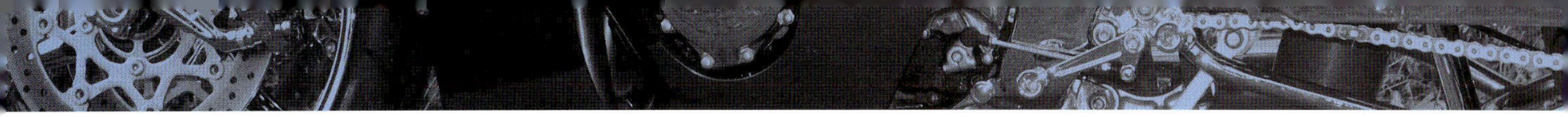

Opposite top: With a set of custom machined spacers, the new wheel just fits within the extended swingarm.

Opposite bottom left: The new 300-millimeter rear tires are monsters in size and sometimes monstrous to mount, as they will not fit most automatic tire-mounting machines.

Opposite bottom right: The front fork tubes are reassembled after 2 inches were cut from each spring to help maintain a low profile.

Above: Halfway there, the rebuilt 'Busa starts to take shape.

Right: The gas tank is striped of paint and molded with Bondo putty for a smoother appearance.

Custom taillight aperture is cut into fiberglass that was plastic-welded onto the tailpiece.

Below: The completed motorcycle, slammed, lowered, and ready for action.

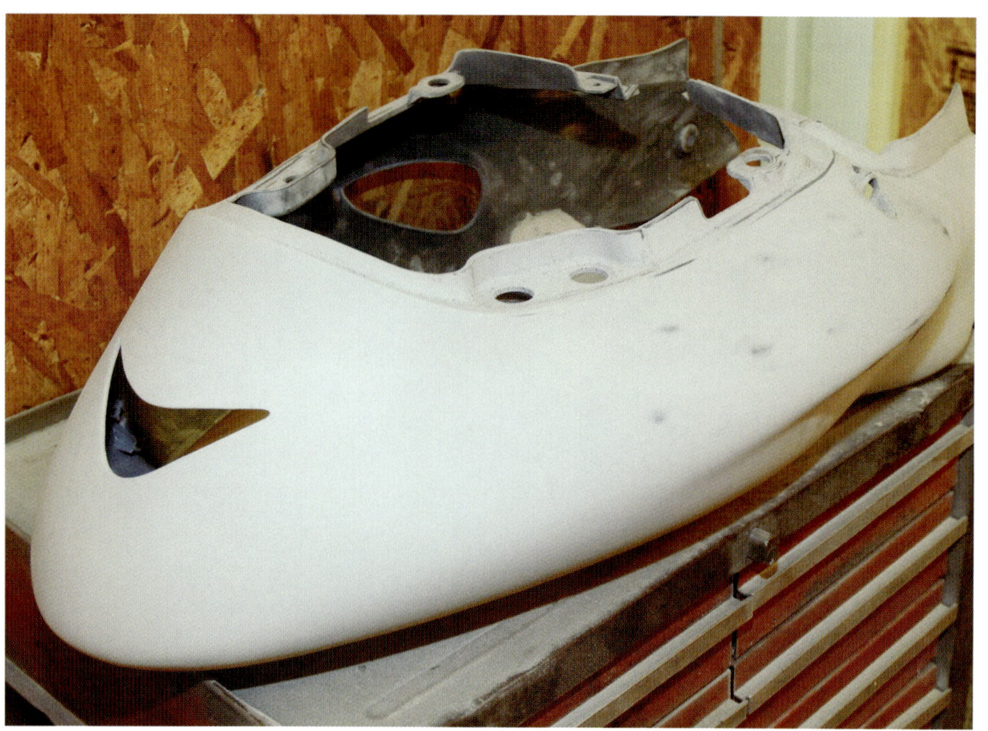

A similar, chevron-shaped hole is cut into the front fairing.

Below: With more than 170 horses on tap, thanks to a 1,400-cc big-bore kit, smoking the rear tire is a simple matter of winding on the throttle.

Above: The air-ride suspension actually provides about 3 inches of travel, meaning the Rick's 'Busa can be ridden comfortably on the streets.
Right: The neighbors may not like you for running a drag race exhaust, but this Brock's megaphone offers the ultimate top-end performance.

Above: Though a small, twin-peg parking stand is utilized for this photo, this bike has a steel skid plate welded to the oil pan and an Air Ride suspension system that makes a sidestand useless.

Left: Note the custom chevron-shaped taillight cutout. Details like these will really set a bike apart from the crowd.

Below: The custom swingarm is stretched 6 inches over stock to help prevent the rear wheel from spinning up under acceleration.

WHY THEY GO LOW—A HISTORY OF SLAMMED STREETBIKES

Originally, it was only professional drag racing motorcycles that rolled on lowered suspension systems. In the early days of quarter-mile motorcycle racing, many riders showed up at the lights on American-made V-Twins rolling on rigid chassis. These frames were pure torture for a rider on the roads, but drag racers soon noticed that their lack of suspension travel meant sure-footed launches at the lights. As Japanese four-cylinder motorcycles began taking over drag racing in the 1970s, their high-revving engines occasionally caused the rear tires to "spin-up," or lose traction, during a launch. This problem was only exacerbated over the following decades as high-performance four-cylinder engines revved to a series of ever-taller redlines. Through trial and a good deal of error, some

This old school Yamaha FZR is tricked and tuned for street racing at Daytona Beach. With the right mods, any sportbike can become competitive.

riders began cutting down their rear shocks or eliminating them altogether, replacing the stock suspension with rigid metal struts. Shortened front forks also helped a bike boogie down the line with less resistance, and fork springs and tubes began to shorten accordingly. Because longer wheelbases meant a motorcycle would launch in a straight line without wobbles, riders began machining extended swingarms to help with traction control. These longer wheel holders worked brilliantly, and today it's unusual to see a serious drag racer rolling without at least bolt-on extensions on their bike. And as thousands of street riders will attest, extended swingarms not only keep the front wheel on the ground and settle the rear, they look cool, too. Just don't try much spirited cornering, though—a lengthened wheelbase makes for slow, sometimes vague steering.

Left: Slammed and lowered mid-1990s Suzuki GSX-R 1100s are still a popular mount for amateur street racers. Above: The twin nitrous bottles cut into this GSX-R gas tank hold enough gas for about four jolts each—just enough to take home a couple of pink slips!

CHAPTER 2
STREET AND TRACK: A NEW KIND OF DUAL-PURPOSE MACHINE

A few years ago, after decades of pushing our luck during wild, irresponsible street rides, a few of my riding buddies had an idea: They'd start taking their sportbikes on organized track day outings, riding in the relative safety of an environment without the dopey car drivers, gravel-strewn turns, and suicidal wildlife of street riding.

On the surface, their decision made all the sense in the world. Out on the twisty, hilly backroads of our native western Pennsylvania, we'd managed to push ourselves and our motorcycles farther than many of us ever imagined. And while we'd explored the limits of control and worked on our cornering and braking skills, it was becoming ever so evident that the streets weren't the best place for what racers call "ten-tenths riding." Choosing stickier tires for our first track day was fun. So was the thought of finally riding flat out, maybe even dragging a knee through the turns without worrying about ending the day in handcuffs.

Less fun was the reality of the situation. After spending a few days choosing a suitable track and enrolling in a novice-level riding school, we started to realize that track

Former racer turned custom sportbike guru Gary Fimiano built this trick Honda track bike, proving that racing iron doesn't have to be ugly.

Kentucky's McCoy Motorsports' handsome take on a street or track drag bike represents the upper end of dual-purpose bikes.

riding brings with it some very specific costs. Most of the serious, dedicated, track day enthusiasts you'll see at your local roadracing circuit appear to have invested a small mortgage in equipment, protective gear, and vehicle transport. In addition to the streetbikes that these guys ride with family or friends, most will tell you they've also invested in track bikes, outfitted them with racing bodywork, reworked suspension systems, and a whole AMA Superbike paddock full of other exotic and costly racing parts. You'll feel even more like a scrub when you watch these guys roll away from the track with their specially outfitted race-only motorcycles parked in the beds of their pickup trucks or stowed neatly away in trailers.

For me, the potential cost outlay was just a bit too much to wrap my helmet around; it seemed downright crazy to go into debt for a race bike that, once stripped of its lights and street accessories, was no longer a form of transportation but a mere toy. And how do you justify the cash outlay for a truck or trailer needed to tow a perfectly functioning motorcycle? It all smacked a little too much of guys who build show bikes that are so blinged out, their

wheels can never meet pavement for fear of dirtying the undercarriages.

Old timers, however, will tell you there's a way around the track day dilemma. Back before the advent of credit cards and disposable incomes, many motorcyclists with a taste for off-street competition riding simply made do with what they had. If bikers wanted to try their hand at drag racing, they simply removed their mufflers and lights and rode to the nearest quarter-mile. During the 1950s and 1960s when a generation of performance-minded British riders built their own homemade café racers for the street, many got their first taste of closed-circuit riding after heading to a local track, taping up their headlamps, and taking their chances with the big boys.

Keep in mind, today's amateur club-racing machines are a far cry from mere modified streetbikes with duct tape over the lights. Your average WERA, Fastraxx, or AMA competition machine has been carefully safety wired so the nuts, bolts, and oil caps stay put; the chain, sprockets, and suspension have likely been carefully reworked for optimum performance; its speedometer, kickstand, lights, horn, and

Above: Genuine track-only rides like this Kawasaki ZX-6R from the California Superbike School are stripped of all lighting equipment, street plastic, and passenger accommodation.

Left: Suzuki's popular and quick GSX-R 1000, given the street-or-strip makeover.

other street necessities were removed long ago; and those extra sticky track day tires wouldn't exactly inspire confidence on a fat street ride during a typically rainy Pennsylvania weekend.

However, many street riders find themselves quickly addicted to the relatively safer and faster environs of track riding, though just as many are baffled by the combination of exhilaration and concern they experience. I've yet to attend a track day where a few riders didn't destroy their machines by misjudging a turn or braking marker, and the experience of watching perfectly fine, $10,000 motorcycles being reduced to wrecks has scared quite a few riders away from the track for good.

The solution? A bike that can do both. Granted, this can be a difficult compromise to reach. Many racers will tell you that a clean cared-for streetbike is no good for even part-time competition use, as most riders are reluctant to risk laying down a flossed-out streetbike, potentially ruining thousands of dollars worth of chrome and hand-rubbed paint. *Super Streetbike* magazine editor Aaron Frank once wrote of how his lap times simply refused to come down during his first year of amateur racing because he'd made the frequent mistake of decorating his racebike with a beautiful, professional-level paint scheme. Only after he acquiesced and sprayed the bike with an ugly flat-black primer finish did he stop worrying about whether he'd emerge from every apex unscathed, and his lap times came down.

Full-time racers will often try and warn prospective track riders away from the notion of building a dual-purpose machine. They opine that track bikes should be used only for competition and that streetbikes offer too many compromises to be fully useful at either job. And though there's truth in the observation that kickstands can occasionally drag during very aggressive cornering, and it can be a genuine hassle—verging on impossibility—to get your track bike home on the public roads after even the slightest fall, many track day enthusiasts not ready to invest in a full-on racing rig would benefit greatly from having a second, dual-purpose bike on hand.

Why? Well, consider how most insurance providers will decline to cover any damage sustained by a streetbike while riding on a closed course. Unless your chosen track day is considered part of a recognized, street-riding instruction school, your streetbike will not be covered if it bites the gravel trap. There are equipment considerations to make as well. Those sticky tires just perfect for reducing your lap times at the track are seldom designed with enough tread to be useful when it rains on the streets, requiring frequent tire changes for anyone planning to make regular visits to the local road race course. It's highly unlikely your streetbike

will be riding hard enough out in traffic to require use of a steering damper, heavyweight springs in your forks, or a revalved shock absorber, but after a few quick sessions around most tracks, many riders find themselves wishing they had made these changes.

However, the specific alterations these machines have been subjected to does not mean an enthusiast can't build a sportbike that's as comfortable on the street as on the track. Best of all, while looking into this project, we spoke with several riders who split their time between street riding and track days, and they tell us that building a dual-purpose bike can be among the most affordable custom sportbike projects around. Why, exactly? Well, insiders say that most track bikes are former street machines that the owners converted for track use after a street spill, or wrecked machines that were picked up for a fraction of their original showroom cost from a salvage yard. It's one of sportbiking's great secrets that insurance providers often relegate a crashed machine to write-off status, even though the damage sustained by said machine is only cosmetic. Often, this is the result of the high replacement costs of factory fairings and other bodywork. A set of stock plastics for, say, a Ducati 999 is so costly, most insurers will simply pay an owner to purchase a new motorcycle rather than bother with replacing the damaged parts.

For our street and track bike, we found a 2000 Honda RC51 that had sustained only a cracked clutch cover, scraped exhaust cans, crash damage to the front fairing and ram air duct, and a gas tank that looked as if it had gone a few rounds with the Freddy Krueger bike in Chapter 1. Though the frames, forks, and wheels on salvage bikes are often badly bent or tweaked, we bribed Eric Ierardo, a mechanic from our local Honda shop to tag along for a thorough diagnosis. When he issued the bike a clean bill of health, we realized that with just 3,400 miles on the clocks, it was a steal at $3,000.

A note of caution: Many salvage yard salesmen possess the honesty level of a used car salesman, so never take them at their word when inquiring about how long a motorcycle may have been sitting unused. Ours was said to have been on the lot for less than a month, but the filthy black engine oil told a different story. Be sure to look at a few telling clues to how long a motorcycle has been sitting idle in the outdoors, including the amount of rust gathered on the drive chain and whether any rodents or insects have had time to build nests on the fairing and running gear.

Keep in mind that a nonsalvage model RC51 would have cost nearly twice as much. With the money saved, I could invest in a host of aftermarket components that would not only increase the big Honda twin's overall track perform-

Shawn Doherty set out to build a bike suited for the street or the track and nearly ended up with a show bike.

ance, it would make the motorcycle ride better on the street and, naturally, look cool in the process. Instead of purchasing a complete set of bodywork for the track and utilizing the stock bodywork for street riding, I managed to track down a clever compromise in the form of a semitransparent vinyl headlight cover from our friends at Lockhart Phillips USA. At $25, it was a hell of a lot cheaper than buying a pickup truck or trailer for my track bike, and because it comes in several colors, it can be custom cut for just about every streetbike. Naturally, this is nowhere near as safe for track riding as removing one's lighting equipment outright, but if you're the type without access to a truck or other transportation, or you enjoy both street riding and the unhindered thrills of a track day, this is a good way to enjoy both.

SHAWN DOHERTY'S TWO-STROKE

Far more popular in Europe and the UK than here in the United States, two-stroke streetbikes nevertheless make excellent track bikes for a number of reasons. Toughening emissions regulations have made the two-stroke a rare sight on most streets, but bikes, including Aprilia's lightweight and very capable RS 250, are common at track days, beloved for their flickability, ease of maintenance, and affordability.

Shawn Doherty of Columbus, Ohio, took a different approach to building a two-stroke track day missile when he found an old 1986 Suzuki RG 500 streetbike and converted it for dual use. "I wanted a cool-looking bike that handled sharp enough and was fast enough to not get left behind on track days, and the RG was perfect," Doherty said.

Replacement bodywork parts and performance accessories abound for this machine, and Doherty picked up a set of full carbon fiber fairings that bolted directly onto the stock mounts. The bodywork is coated in a sheen of House of Kolor candy cobalt blue and then clear-coated for a lasting shine. A set of small 55-watt headlights peek through the nosecone, providing just enough light to be street legal, but not enough exposed glass surface to be a problem for track day scrutiny.

Design school graduate Doherty designed and then manufactured his own rearsets on a milling machine, opt-

Right: Suzuki's RG 500 was a popular track day mount in Europe, but it's a rare sight stateside.

Below: Tiny LED taillight and halogen fronts make this two-stroker legal, if only just barely.

Though few track day addicts would make this big an investment in a race bike, this Duck has plenty of street flash.

ing to replace the Suzuki's conventional forks with a complete Showa inverted front end from a 2004 GSX-R 1000. Doherty said the machine's 360-pound running weight is no match for the GSX-R radial brakes, which help the machine stop in record time. This was not an easy conversion to complete, the owner warns, requiring a custom-made set of triple clamps, hand-machined wheel spacers to accommodate the wider GSX-R wheel, and careful positioning of the front end within the triple clamps. A true do-it-yourselfer, Doherty also vulcanized a gas tank from a Suzuki GS 500 commuter bike, attaching a Pingel petcock for fueling, while at the rear he's running a WP suspension shock absorber with adjustable preload, rebound, and damping, and a braced swingarm to hold the 5.5-inch wide GSX-R rear wheel. The two-stroker breathes through reworked Mikuni carbs with rotary valves, Lance jets, and air filters channeling oxygen to the chromed Jolly Moto canister exhausts. A glance at the custom aluminum dash reveals only a lap timer and tachometer—speedometers tend to only distract us on the track!

Despite the level of brightwork deployed on this machine, Doherty's is a particularly clever example of a motorcycle that's practical enough for the street, yet fast and tweakable enough to hold its own at any track day. Used examples of mid-1980s Suzuki two-stroke street machines

can be had for only a few thousand dollars, meaning replacement parts are both plentiful and cheap. It's only impractical bits are the one-off carbon bodywork, which would cost plenty to replace in the event of a low-side crash, but you can't beat it for light weight and good looks.

SUPERBIKE ITALIA'S DUCATI 996

Some would say the very idea of using an expensive, exclusive, Italian superbike like a Ducati 996 for a track day tool is like using a $300 Calphalon frying pan to make grilled cheese sandwiches. And though the possibility of crashing an exotic beauty like this will keep most owners as far away from the dangers of a track as most can get, many owners have found the machines perfect for roadracing use due to their unparalleled handling.

"I could have used a lot of cheaper bikes when I started out, but you'll save yourself lots of time on the track trying to sort out your suspension and cornering by just using a bike that already handles like a race bike," explained Ken Hall, owner of Superbike Italia in Lemont, Illinois.

Hall, a former jet aircraft technician, built, or should we say *built up*, this 2003 model for use on the street and track, figuring the bike provided a suitable platform for displaying many of the exotic carbon fiber and performance parts his shop imports from Italy. Fans of World Superbike rac-

Right: Sportbike Italia combines beauty, functionality, and some serious carbon fiber on their flagship Ducati 996, including facing-style radial brakes.

Below: This aftermarket fairing utilizes a tiny halogen headlamp. Smaller light means fewer risks on the track.

ing will immediately recognize the featherweight Technosel seat unit on Ken's machine, a popular item for professional racers that's rarely used on the street. The machine is awash in more carbon fiber than a NASA parts cupboard, shaving about 22 pounds from the motorcycle's already diminutive dry weight. The front carbon fender is vented to allow cooling of the Brembo brake disc during hot laps, while the fairing inners, bellypan, tank strap, and single-sided swingarm cover are all made of the ultra lightweight resin. The stock clutch has been beefed up with Barnett springs and a special red anodized pressure plate from Italy's Moto Corse. Twin carbon mufflers from Arrow add an additional eleven top-end ponies to the Ducati's 121-horsepower rating, and the enlarged airbox also helps speed things along in the aspiration department. A custom front fairing sports only a single tiny halogen headlight, a common modification for riders who like the option of street riding combined with the relative safety of a small headlight for the track. Hall notes that the halogen bulb will also come in handy if he ever considers endurance racing.

Hall has installed a set of stiffer aftermarket fork springs from Race Tech, though many street riders say stiffening the front suspension can have its drawbacks, creating a ride that is too harsh for relaxed riding but flawless on the track. Whether to make this adjustment is up to an individual builder, who may want to consider how much of either type of riding they plan to do. There's also an adjustable steering damper in place on Hall's Ducati, as

A genuine Technosel seat as used in the World Superbike series. A carbon tank strap helps protect paint.

seen on most race bikes. These dampers are a considerable investment for any street rider. As most modern sportbikes arrive from the factory equipped with at least a nonadjustable model, it's up to the individual whether the cost outlay is worthwhile. The Ohlins shock absorber is full adjustable and just as it came stock on the Ducati 996 SPS model on which this machine is based. It saves track day enthusiasts the expense of having to purchase and install an aftermarket damper better suited to track riding. Likewise, the five-spoke Marchesini alloy wheels are far lighter than their cast counterparts, saving weight and expense over having to upgrade.

Many riders with machines of this quality will also invest the $600 necessary to maintain a set of track-only fairings and fenders, considering the expense of replacing or repairing costly stock panels. Hall, however, offers full bodywork repair at his shop, so patching up any track day dings or dents isn't much of an issue.

Creating a street/track bike of this caliber is fairly simple, as most of the accessories that make Hall's Ducati special are bolt-ons that any mechanic of average talents can attach in a matter of hours. There are clearly cheaper alternatives available for track riding, but with used Ducatis from the 916/996/998 series coming onto the used market for around $8,000, they do make excellent dual-purpose bikes, requiring fewer modifications than most streetbikes.

THE BUILD

Roadracing experts say there are better handling twin-cylinder sportbikes on the market than Honda's RC51, with Aprilia's RSV Mille and Ducati's 916/996/998 series springing to mind. However, unlike those exotic repli-racers, Honda has produced far more units of its flagship twin sportbike, meaning used models are plentiful on the used market. Ours being a rolling refugee from a salvage yard made for a cheap platform to build from, though it must be said that buying wrecked sportbikes is an inexact science, one best undertaken with plenty of caution. Veterans of the salvage bike trade warn newcomers of hidden defects in otherwise clean-looking bikes—like bent or cracked frames, distorted wheels that no longer run true, and fork irregularities that never seem to surface until you're deep into a fast corner, wondering why the rear wheel doesn't seem to be tracking in the same line as the front!

There are solutions to these common problems with wrecked motorcycles. One is the computer-assisted frame alignment services of GMD Computrack, a nationwide chassis straightening service originally used exclusively by roadracers. The thick, twin-spar aluminum frames cradling most modern sportbike engines are relatively rigid, tough designs, but they can be knocked out of plumb by even a slight contact with the pavement or other immovable object. This doesn't mean a bike can't be ridden any longer, but for

Found at a salvage yard for under $3,000, this 2000 Honda RC51 was in better shape than it appears.

The worst damage included this curious, hatchet-shaped puncture in the gas tank and an abrasion on the other side.

it to again reach its true performance potential, a visit to one of GMD's ride-in service centers is well worth the expense.

Fortunately, the massive frame rails on modern sportbikes do an excellent job of protecting the engines and transmissions, which usually escape crashes relatively unscathed. Our Honda project bike suffered only a slight, cosmetic dent in the left-side frame rail and a ruptured magnesium clutch cover. There were several aftermarket items available to replace the clutch cover, but we opted to search the classified section of *Motorcyclist Magazine*, where we found several used parts distributors with used models for sale. A new gasket was installed, the dirty and very well used engine oil and filter were replaced, and we were back in business for less than $150.

The scrapes sustained along the right-side fairing lowers in this motorcycle's near-fatal low-side were, on close inspection, only cosmetic in nature. Rather than shell out the bucks to replace the fairing or have it professionally

Left: Jardine carbon fiber slip-on pipes sound wonderful, but serious scrapes means they'll have to go.

Below: Looking like it just went through the gravel trap at Laguna Seca, this bike needs some serious upgrades.

repainted, we took a cue from many money-conscious amateur racers and simply ordered replacement stickers for the ones that had been damaged. Honda will sell you high-quality replacements for around $145 per side, and these glossy, easy-to-apply babies are slick and durable enough to require no clear-coating for years of all-weather use. Plenty of aftermarket firms, including England's Image Works (www.the-image-works.co.uk), offer similar decals kits for a fraction of the price.

Honda's RC51 is one of the few modern sportbikes to utilize a full steel gas tank. Ours had suffered the misfortune of a deep, slotted gash that appeared to have penetrated all the way through to the inner liner. Disconnecting the fuel pump and all the venting and fuel feed lines was a pain, but after carefully working the fittings loose, off they came. A competent bodyman, custom motorcycle painter and bodywork expert Ron Tonetti, was able to patch the baseball-sized dent in the right side and patch the gash. Ron, of Pittsburgh's North Hills Cycle, used automotive dent-puling tools to pull the caved-in surface back to plumb, but he said many builders will simply plumb all the venting and gas flow holes and use high-pressure compressed air to force out a dent. To patch the irregularities, Ron used fiberglass Bondo putty to smooth over the uneven surfaces, sanding and reapplying the compound until smooth again.

We could have purchased a fully painted replacement RC51 gas tank new from Honda for $850 or perused an Internet auction like eBay for a used model retailing any-

To ward off any future crash damage, Eric installs a set of frame sliders from Lockhart Phillips.

The frame sliders use an extralong motor mounting bolt, and they attach in minutes.

where from $400 to $500, depending on condition. However, we figured a skilled bodyman could help us keep the original parts, repaired and fully painted, with factory-matched colors from Colorite Paints for just $350.

Our Honda was five years old when spotted, looking sad and unloved in a salvage yard, though the Dunlop D207 tires looked as if they had enough tread left to last another 2,000 miles. That is, if we wanted to end up sliding on our butts after the first turn. While restoring a salvage motorcycle for either street or, especially, track use, you can't be too careful when it comes to choosing the right tires. All modern radial motorcycle hoops have a manufacturing date stamped into the sidewalls near the inflation rate info block, and experts warn of using any tire that's three years old or older. Though a tire can appear perfectly solid to the naked eye, chemical compounds can begin to break down with

Left: Hardened plastic bobbins, also from Lockhart Phillips, were attached to the swingarm and handlebar ends. For only a few bucks, they can potentially save thousands in track day damage.

Below: A Hotbodies Racing undertail bolts onto the rear subframe and includes flush clear-lens lights, which are less susceptible to damage.

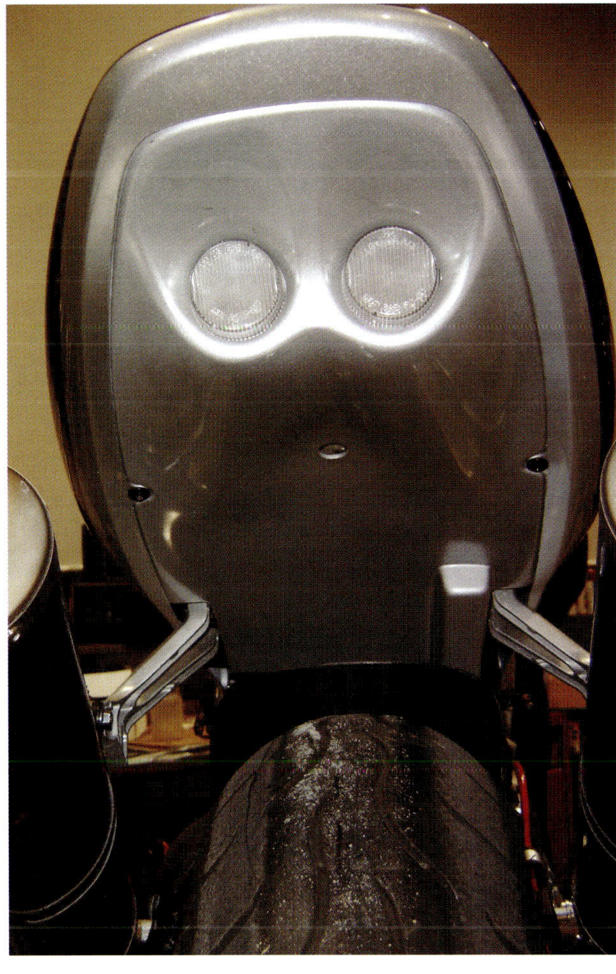

constant exposure to the atmosphere, and dry rot can set in before most riders realize it.

Because we didn't plan to compete in any actual club races with this machine, we opted for a set of Supermaxx sport-touring radials from Maxxis tires. It's one of the best-kept secrets in sportbiking that hypersport tires designed for track days and street riding are generally excellent at the former but seldom last long enough to experience much of the latter. For track day riding at the level enjoyed by the average rider, sport touring compounds like the Supermaxx provide more than enough traction while retaining enough tread to dissipate rain and long-distance street rides.

We thought long and hard about whether or not to change the stock RC51 aluminum alloy wheels. Modern sportbike rims are far lighter than they were just a decade ago, and are sturdy enough to withstand repeated tire changes without sustaining damage. But suspension experts tell us that eliminating unsprung weight on a motorcycle is one of the best ways to improve a bike's handling, convincing us to opt for a set of aftermarket rims from California's RC Components. Their spun aluminum rims are a couple of pounds lighter than the stock wheels and in a polished aluminum finish, looking like something from a World Superbike paddock. The wheels mounted in about a half-hour, utilizing the stock spacers in the front; the rear required the installation of two RC spacers, which fit inside the stock wheel bearings with help from a small rubber mallet. RC Components even offers at-home builders a toll-free

Here, Steve reattaches the replacement front fairing. Plastic can often be sourced secondhand from salvage yards.

customer service line with free advice on installation, sprocket choices, etc.

One aspect of track riding that street riders find the most difficult to adjust to is the rapid, almost frenzied, level of braking required. Unlike street riding, where most twisty section of road are interrupted by miles of boring, twist-the-throttle-and-sightsee straights, track riders are constantly braking, accelerating, and leaning their way around a circuit. And while most sportbike brakes are more than up to the challenge, it's cost-effective and smart to modify your street and track machine with aftermarket brakes.

Though full aftermarket calipers and sexy wave rotors are an option for a higher-end rebuild, we received an excellent upgrade in the form of a set of Kevlar brake lines from California's Galfer Braking Systems. These sleek, plastic-coated lines provide far superior braking for bikes using their stock calipers, because the Kevlar material forces greater pressure on the hydraulic fluid, getting it from your master cylinder to the rotors even faster. Galfer also provided a set of full racing brake pads for both the front and rear wheels, providing a smooth, progressive shearing off of speed on the street or track. Finally, we finished off with a matching red clutch line also from Galfer, the complete setup retailing for just under $400.

The Honda RC51 is said to have some of the toughest suspension this side of an off-road vehicle, though a rider's weight and riding style can often prove the stock springs to be deficient. It's no secret that modern sportbikes are generally designed to fit tiny test riders who seldom weigh more than 140 pounds in a full suit of leathers. This means an average-sized American motorcyclist will quickly find the limits of his or her suspension components the first time they try riding their streetbike on street suspension settings at a track day.

McCoy Motorsports supplied these trick mirror blanks. Track bikes must remove their mirrors, remember!

But to bypass this regulation, we're running an on-board rearview camera from MotoCam, which mounts with a simple wiring harness that fits into the tail section.

The MotoCam lens is attached to the undertail using zip ties threaded through holes drilled in the unit; wiring runs inside the bodywork.

One of the most rewarding modifications we've made to our streetbikes involves upgrading the front forks with heavyweight springs from the lines of Race Tech, Ohlins, or Hyperpro. Any of these cheap (around $100 per set) spring kits will allow riders to increase the preload settings on their forks to suit a heavier or more aggressive rider, and the springs are generally offered in increments of density to suit everything from a cheeseburger-friendly street rider to your average Valentino Rossi fan at the track. Installed in about an hour by a competent trained mechanic, heavier fork springs cured our RC51 of that strange—and, not to mention, confidence-sapping—pogo-stick feeling we had experienced during our first track run.

Aftermarket exhaust systems are the most popular modification for sportbikes, adding noise, which makes riders happy, and just a tiny bit of performance. Full systems comprising header pipes and connecting mufflers—often referred to as "full race systems"—offer the greatest bolt-on horsepower gains, though these also require airbox modifications and careful recalibration of a fuel injection map to achieve full effect. As the RC51 requires a two-in-two sys-tem, a full race exhaust would cost nearly twice as much as those designed for four-cylinder bikes. Instead, we went with a set of brilliant carbon fiber bolt-ons from Eastern Europe's Akrapovic exhausts. Our technicians Eric and Steve had enough experience working with Honda motorcycles that they had a few clever performance tricks up their sleeves that would help maximize the engine's output without splashing cash on a full system.

The folks at Honda, for some reason, sought to install what's commonly known as a "soft" rev limiter on the RC51's engine. This cuts power at around 9,500 rpm, though in-the-know mechanics say this system can safely be disabled by cutting two wires from the emissions module to the fuel injection mapping box. This allows the engine to rev safely to around 10,500 rpm before the override system cuts power. There's also a set of rubber block-off plates in the airflow hoses mounted atop the cylinder head that can be removed, freeing up additional airflow to the airbox and bypassing the emission valves. These simple 10-second modifications add around 9 rear-wheel horsepower at the Honda's top end, and makes for a freer breathing engine.

continued on page 61

Above: The display will bolt atop this flash Cycle Cat billet aluminum triple clamp. Cycle Cat clip-ons also feature trick adjustable angle mounts for comfort.

Left: The 5-inch LCD screen contains clever light-gathering technology that keeps the rear-view clear at night.

Above: Before the side fairings are reattached, Eric drills a 2-inch-diameter hole for the frame sliders.

Right: Custom anodized red endcaps are included from Lockhart Phillips and look the business!

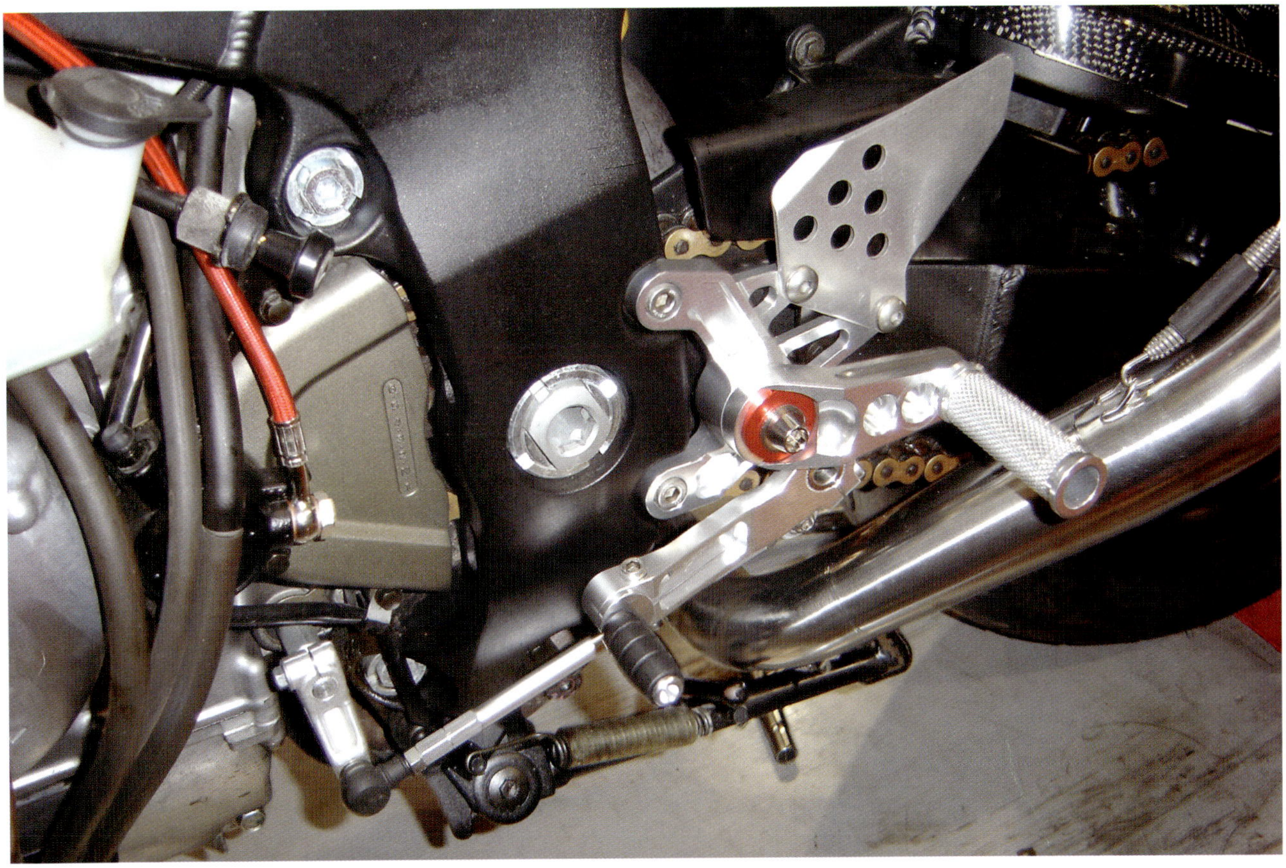

Above: Tall riders often complain of limited leg room on race replica bikes like the RC. Cycle Cat's rearsets offer a solution.

Left: Using the stock heel plates, these billet beauties bolt directly on using stock brake and shift linkage. Multiple adjustments mean no track day leg cramps.

Right: Galfer's Kevlar brake lines add even more oomph to the stock Nissin stoppers.

Below: An Akrapovic slip-on carbon exhaust system sounds and breathes well and bolts easily to the stock headpipe using the Honda can hangers.

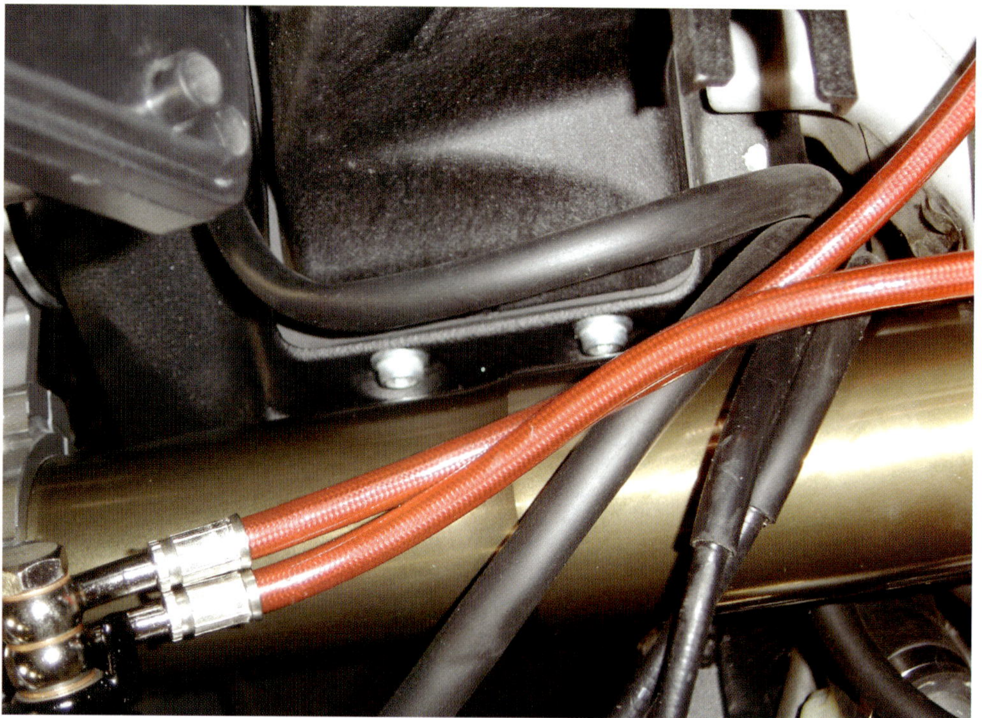

continued from page 56

Along with the Akrapovic cans, we're talking dyno figures around 125 horsepower from an otherwise stock engine.

As we mentioned earlier in this chapter, turn signals would not be necessary for a full-on racebike, but for a motorcycle we intend to ride on the street and the track, we'll still need to maintain all the street-legal amenities that make the boyz in blue happy. To that effect, we've added a set of nifty flush-mount turn signals from Lockhart Phillips (about $20). Much smaller than the stock indicators and bereft of those awkward-looking stalks that place the amber light out away from the motorcycle, the flush-mount signals stand a far better chance of surviving an impact than stock models. They install in just seconds by removing the stock indicators, then disconnecting the two wires feeding the small auxiliary bulb. After reconnecting the wires, we cut the existing turn signal mounting hole with a Dremmel tool, widening the aperture just enough for the new LP backing

Right: Eric bolts down the rebuilt and painted gas tank atop the airbox, which now sports K&N filters. Below: A Dynojet Power Commander wired into the ECU, Eric maps the freed-up RC on the dyno.

With the soft rev-limiter disabled and the EPA restrictions gone, we're looking at 125 horses at the rear wheel.

plate to fit. Though some flush-mount signals mount with simple double-sided adhesive, ours offered a sturdier design, the clear face lens bolting on with a single Phillips screw.

Short of purchasing a full set of race plastics, which would allow us to disconnect our street lighting equipment, we instead installed a clever stopgap modification. Lockhart Phillips offers a slick headlight mesh from EFX. Sold in 12x15-inch sheets for around $25, this mesh material can be applied directly to factory headlights with no adhesive, and allows light to pass through a system of tiny holes while protecting the headlight from disintegrating in the event of a crash. Though this would hardly pass a race teach session, it's just fine for the sort of casual track day riding we have in mind.

Left: Lightweight, spun aluminum, RC Components Daytona wheels are mounted using the stock front spacers and billet RC spacers at the rear.

Below: The polished Daytona rims are a couple of pounds lighter than the stock RC wheels making for quicker steering on street or track.

The Maxxis Supermax tires are the perfect choice for street riders curious about the track. They're long lasting and sticky, with the right combination of durability and poise.

Thanks to advances in LED technology, there are more options available for riders looking to customize their sportbike's taillight than can fit on an average shop shelf. We liked the clean lines and simplicity of the Hotbodies Supersport undertail system ($190), a sleek, single-piece unit that bolts to the underside of the RC51's subframe with four small screws in minutes. The unit also includes a set of inlaid taillights with highly visible red lenses, though an LED option is available for later models. The undertray also makes for an easy cleanup of the Honda's rear end, making chain lube and road grime a simple wipe-away matter.

Down below, we lightened our track-and-street bike's load by bolting on a pair of Carbon Works fenders from Lockhart Phillips (around $425 per set). Complete with a glossy clearcoat finish, the front fender weighs a good quarter-pound less than the plastic stock unit. The front bolted easily into place using the factory hardware, while the rear hugger was a bit more involved. Because Honda did not see fit to attach a hugger to the RC51 in 2000, there was no

mounting point provided on the swingarm for the rear fender. The Lockhart Phillips kit included an adhesive strap and a small bolt that threaded into the metal strap that attaches to the swingarm with hand pressure in minutes.

Many streetbikes you'll see wadded up in the paddock at a track day suffer unnecessary damage to expensive frames and running gear because manufacturers, for some unknown reason, have largely failed to equip sportbikes with any protective hardware. The metal bar-end caps on your sportbike will protect your hands and handlebars in a crash, but they're not designed to survive more than one impact. To this end, we equipped our machine with a full complement of Lockhart Phillips protective hardware, including hardened carbon/metal bar ends ($40) and matching frame sliders. Their stalks done up in a snazzy red anodized finish, the engine guards ($99) mount to the engine at the stiff motor mount points. The billet aluminum end caps are replaceable and match a set of carbon swingarm sliders ($40) designed to protect the chain, rear

Carbon Works carbon fiber fenders from Lockhart Phillips look trick and shave even more weight from the RC's 498-pound wet weight.

brake caliper, and other costly bits in a crash. These units bolt on so quickly and work so well, it remains one of the wonders of the motorcycle industry that manufacturers haven't started providing them as factory equipment.

Our Honda project bike would definitely need a set of replacement mirrors for road use, but for track days the rear-views would have to be removed time and time again. One fun and, we must admit, wholly over-the-top way around this problem was to install a rear-view camera unit from Moto-Cam. This allows us to narrow our bike's profile by removing the mirrors for good, filling in the fairing holes with a set of groovy little, black anodized billet aluminum mirror blanks from Gregg's Customs. Instead, the MotoCam model 400 mounts in place using a threaded bar that fits through the top clamp fork bolt. A ball-and-joint mounting system allows the 5-inch LED screen to be mounted conveniently beneath the Honda's fairing stay. It required a few minutes of adjustment before the screen cleared the instrument panel, leaving a full view of the tachometer and digital speedo. We then ran the

power cable underneath the gas tank and zip-tied the lines to the frame and battery. The power module fit neatly beneath the seat alongside the electronics black box, while the rear-view camera lens, about the diameter of a travel-size deodorant can, was mounted to the underside of the undertray using zip-ties.

At only $400 complete for the cheapest version, the MotoCam provided a clear, wide-angle view of the action behind us, which was a real handy tool on the track where we usually only knew we were about to be passed from the noise from an approaching bike. The camera even attracts ambient light, which means it works perfectly even at night, suffering very little vibration after we added a small bit of foam rubber padding to the camera lens in its rear mounting.

When we wheeled it off the work stands, we were satisfied that we'd created a streetbike with the looks and performance to hang with the fat guys and, at the same time, a track bike that wouldn't be hamstrung in its performance by being too pretty, fragile, or impractical. And it didn't cost nearly as much as even the cheapest trailer or pick-up truck!

Completed and ready for the canyons or the track, the project RC proves a dual-purpose sportbike doesn't have to be impractical or expensive. Besides its salvage certificate, this reconditioned 125-horsepower screamer is even better than new.

RESOURCE GUIDE

Lockhart Phillips
Streetbike and track day accessories
(800) 221-7291
lockhartphillipsusa.com

MotoCam
Rearview cameras
1-877-MOTOCAM
themotocam.com

RC Components
Spun aluminum sportbike wheels
(800) 513-6838
rccomponents.com

West Hills Honda
Motorcycle dyno tuning, bike building, parts
(412) 262-2200
westhills-honda.com

Hotbodies Racing
Undertails, fairings
(800) 555-2805
hotbodiesracing.com

Galfer Braking Products
Brake pads, Kevlar brake lines, rotors
(800) 685-6633
galferusa.com

Maxxis tires
Track day and street tires
maxxis.com

CHAPTER 3
BLING MACHINES: FORM OCCASIONALLY WHOOPS FUNCTION'S ASS

Even the most dedicated fan of choppers will occasionally find themselves eyeballing an episode of their favorite custom motorcycle TV show with a recurring question on their mind: Who rides these crazy things? If you've ever watched in fascination as a custom motorcycle builder expends gallons of sweat equity in a machine that seems to place drop-dead gorgeous looks over passing-lane rideability, a show machine with polished and plated surfaces that hate rain as much as a California surfer, a motorcycle that takes more chances than a stunt rider with a police chief father, well, this is the machine for you.

Until just recently, over-the-top bling machines were mainly the property of custom chopper and cruiser builders.

Many of the machines gracing the trophy stands at bike shows and TV programs were runners only in the most open sense of the word. Many were started and run just enough to be seen doing so on camera, while in the 1960s it wasn't uncommon for builders to enter bikes on the show circuit without pistons or flywheels in the engines! Thankfully, the new generation of extreme custom sportbikes are designed to ride with as much style as they have wild looks.

The most popular custom alteration separating bling bikes from other creations of the tuner nation are their oversized rear tires. Veterans of this scene claim the desire to beef up a sportbike's rear end originated from the street drag racing scene, a place where wider rubber means instant trac-

Voodoo Customs went full bore with this GSX-R 1000 Suzuki, a show-winner fo' sho'.

67

A digital speedometer is mounted in the gas tank featuring an endurance racing gas cap.

A 300-series rear wheel leaves little room for accessories, so the license plate is mounted vertically.

Left: Chroming your top clamp can cause occasional blindness, but custom fans say it's worth the risk.

Below: Instant bling. Take one Ducati-powered Bimota, DB4, dip liberally in carbon, and hit the streets.

Kawasaki's ZX-9R in extreme street custom form makes an excellent show bike.

tion. But like many custom movements, the practice of adapting a wider-than-stock rim to your streetbike quickly became a game of "whose rim is wider" with fabricators experimenting with all sorts of wicked hub, rim, and swingarm combinations to be known as the King of Phat. It didn't take long for the motorcycle parts industry to join in the scrap, serving up lane-wide rubber to fit an increasingly expanding rear tire market. As a result, the stock, 190-millimeter rims on a Suzuki Hayabusa or even the 200-millimeter tires adorning a Kawasaki ZX-12 look downright puny in comparison to their aftermarket brothers.

Mike McCoy, co-owner of Kentucky's McCoy Motorsports, says the current craze for extreme fat tires is both a blessing and curse. He was experimenting with ways to adapt a 300-millimeter tire to a Yamaha YZF-R6 back in 2003, and says the effects the ultrawide rim had on the previously nimble supersport weren't exactly inspiring. "The bike really felt like it was going to drop flat on its side every time you ride it around a corner," McCoy recalls. "The tires really start to flatten out in cornering at that kind of width, so you really need to know what you're doing riding one."

Apparently, the effect the rim width had on handling wasn't much of an issue with sportbike fans, who have flocked to McCoy's Pikeville shop for elaborate phat tire conversion kits. Not satisfied with just 240-millimeter (or 6.5-inch) rims, customers are now paying out some serious cash for trick kits that allow room for a 300-millimeter tire, replete with a dense, single-sided swingarm requiring two final-drive chains and a jackshaft to transfer power to the pavement. There are several reputable firms offering wide tire kits to fit most popular sportbikes (listings can be found at the end of this chapter in a complete resource guide) and this chapter features a complete ground-up bling bike build from one of the best, Florida's Custom Sportbike Concepts.

Builders will tell you it takes more to build a show-winning bling bike than just a rear end that looks like a prop from a Ludacris video. At what many call the highest level of sportbike customizing, proficiency at custom painting and smoothing plastic bodywork, some sheetmetal working prowess and mad skills with the welding torch are also necessary. Over the past few years, we've watched as the bar has been continually raised on the sportbike show scene. Where a polished aluminum frame and rims might have once won you a trophy (or a trophy girl) a few years back, today's serious show winners seldom arrive with anything short of a fully chromed frame and swingarm. Painters are taking chances with anodizing metals for wicked effect, laying down tinted finishes on chromed wheels, chassis, and detail parts.

With a $4,000 paint scheme involving nude women, dollar bills, and tribal designs, you couldn't miss this custom Gixxer in a crowd.

Bling on the cheap. A finish of automotive paint, a radically extended swingarm, and dayglow detailing makes this 1995 EXUP Yamaha a winner.

Who says Italian bikes have to cost an arm and a plate of pasta? This Bimota SB8R custom was built for under $15,000.

"For a lot of guys, it's all a matter of going to the shows, looking at what everybody else is doing, and then thinking real long and hard about how to beat them," said Tim Brown, owner of Atlanta's Alum-A-Chrome, one of the world's best known tuner bike shops. Brown has managed to create amazing theme bikes at his shop, incorporating artwork from popular horror flicks and eventually graduating toward three-dimensional design elements, eye-popping spinner rims, and on-board DVD players showing the same films that adorn his rides.

Naturally, this is one level of craftsmanship where a builder's budget is nearly as important as the mechanical and artistic skills they bring to the lift stand. Spinner rims with custom computer-designed and CNC-milled spokes don't come cheap, and it doesn't take long on the show circuit to locate an unfinished project bike that some poor builder has abandoned because of cost overruns. But this is, after all, the rarefied air where Hahn Racecraft twin turbochargers are bolted into $30,000 exotic Italian superbikes; where a set of Cycle Cat custom-milled billet aluminum triple clamps are *de rigeur* and a pair of $5,000 World Superbike-spec carbon-fiber rims are considered an entry level accessory.

But sometimes, beating the competition means having a fertile imagination more than a deep back account. Over the past few years we've seen some very awe-inspiring custom pro street machines created out of the remnants of bikes that many riders wouldn't bother rebuilding. When Italian superbike firm Bimota took a nose-dive a few years back, the existing stock of new machines in the United States suddenly dropped in value like an Escalade with a bullet hole in the driver's side door. Blisteringly fast machines powered by retuned Japanese and Italian powerplants, the Bimota name was synonymous with cutting edge technology and farout styling at a time when most Japanese streetbikes had all the style of a pair of gray suede Hush Puppies.

One of the most famous custom Bimotas ever devised came from the exclusive design studios of Japanese tuner Shin Kondo. Kondo reworked a 200-model Bimota SB8R into a track and show machine—replete with a 140-horse-power engine, a $4,000 tunnel-port titanium exhaust header, and a velvet seat from Italy's Moto Corse. It made the pages of enthusiast magazines in five countries.

When I saw a stock SB8R for sale for about half of its original $26,000 price a few years ago, I jumped instantly, tearing into the Suzuki TL 1000R-powered sportster. My goal

Left: Though the carbon fiber bodywork appears to be inlaid in green, it's only a film of polyurethane clearcoat with House of Kolor green paint added.

Below: Bikes like this can be picked up relatively cheaply these days and make excellent, fast, pro street customs.

Above: It didn't cost a fortune to trick out this 1991 GSX-R 1100, just lots of style and imagination.

Right: Rearview mirrors have been swapped for miniature LCD screens for the Playstation console under the gas tank.

was to at least partially recreate the beauty of the machine that Shin Kondo had completed. Though his costs were upward of $60,000, I had picked up a few tricks to knock that figure down considerably. Kondo's SB8RC, as it was dubbed, featured the Bimota's stock carbon fiber frame and bodywork, done up in an unbelievable green carbon inlay.

A local Harley-Davidson builder, Ron Tonetti, hepped me to the fact that Kondo's pricey green carbon bodywork was actually just a bit of House of Kolor green mixed with polyurethane clearcoat, then spray-gunned over plain old carbon fiber. For about as much as it costs to spray a set of fenders, Tonetti splashed on the deep green to my Bimota, creating a machine that looks like it cost the price of a Tokyo high-rise, and for less than thirteen grand. All over the place, we're finding similar approaches to creating mind-blowing customs out of little or nothing. Jose

Rodriguez of Superbike Concepts in Stuart, Florida, walked away with all the top trophies at the prestigious (and very hard to win) Palm Beach, Florida, Bike Show for building a bling machine characterized by wild, one-of-a-kind body-work, not high-dollar technical gadgetry. His show-winning machine was based on a 2003 Suzuki Hayabusa, slammed and lowered to the pavement thanks to an air-ride suspension system, a hand-crafted underseat exhaust system, a 300-series rear rim, yards of show chrome, and a truly inspired reworking of the 1300's bodywork, which involved dozens of three-dimensional scales and spikes topping bright orange lizard-scale paint. Rodriguez's scaly orange 'Busa didn't cost six figures or more to construct, and he won't be paying off parts bills well into his retirement. Instead, the machine proves that with enough imagination and skill, custom sportbikes can push the boundaries as far as any chopper guys, if not farther.

PLAYAS' STATION

One of the most common gripes heard by a winning show-bike owner is that the guy with the most money naturally wins. While that can easily be said to be the case when it comes to superbike racing or poker tournaments, it simply doesn't apply when creating your dream bike. That's because building a machine that captures your particular vision of a custom sportbike can be pulled off with a lot less money than most riders think.

Take this funky, blue, stretch Suzuki GSX-R, for example. We spotted it rolling through the pit lane during an

Who needs a shock absorber when you could have an electronic fish tank with "fish" swimming inside?

An extended swingarm, a fur-covered seat, and enough attitude for miles.

Shane McCoy test-riding one of his shop's wickedly fast project bikes.

AMA Superbike round at Mid-Ohio a while back, and even though it was built for less than the price of a new stock 'Busa, the owner had trouble finding a parking spot for his baby because of the crowds it generated. Marcus Streeter's ride is basically a 1992 GSX-R 1100, a motorcycle so over-shadowed by its lighter, sharper-handling younger brother, the GSX-R 1000, that decent used models can be found for as little as $3,500 in good running condition. Starting with just such a bike, Streeter constructed a machine that's com-fortable cutting through the traps at the drag strip and flashy enough to turn heads at bike night.

Some of the custom touches Streeter happened upon are sheer genius in a funky, ghetto-fabulous kind of way. The joystick controller attached to the gas tank with Velcro is from a Sony Play Station 2 module that's wired into the bike's electrical system. The PS2 is actually hidden in the space inside the right-side fairing, while Streeter mounted a set of tiny, 3x5-inch LCD screens in the rear-view mirror consoles that display the gaming images for his passenger to see.

Think that's not quite crazy enough? Well, because this machine is meant to burn fuel in a straight line rather than in the twisties, Streeter, like many street draggers, realized that suspension travel at the rear end was only slowing his machine's progress. So out came the stock Kayaba shock absorber, replaced by a set of rigid lowering struts. This makes the big Suzook launch like a scaled gorilla in a straight line, and the modification—which cost less than $300—also left room for the installation of a fake fish tank in place of the shock, occupied by a small school of battery-operated tropical fish.

The sheepskin seat cover matches the pale white flames on a pastel blue paint scheme, while a Kerker open drag racing header lets the world know Streeter has arrived. The stock Suzuki frame has been polished to a high buff. Chrome plating was applied to the lowered forks and wheels, while the Hahn Racing swingarm has a 6-inch extension. Overall, this bike simply rocks, rocking points for its inventive use of found custom touches and gritty street detail.

WEB OF STYLE

Shane McCoy and brother Mike have a reputation for breaking the bank when building their signature wild and wide custom sportbikes. It was Mike who first started experimenting with radical changes to the suspension, wheelbase, and tire widths of Yamaha R-1s a few years back, and as customers began demanding ever more outrageous rides, the brothers combined their talents on the blue and red Spider-Man-themed bike seen in this chapter. Built

from the remains of a streetbike destroyed in a collision with a car, the 2004 R-1 has been turned into a showbike with some serious drag strip potential.

The whole shebang starts on the McCoy Motorsports design terminal, where the brothers create a detailed 3D map of just how the finished bike should look. That eliminates any potential communications errors between them and their favorite painters at Color Zone. Colors play a very large part in this bike's appeal, evidenced by the revolutionary application of blue and red powdercoating on the extended Trac Dynamics swingarm, frame, and brake components. Far more durable than paint and able to withstand the effects of regular road use, the McCoys swear by the powdercoating process, which was used as a basecoat for the elaborate spiderweb mural as well.

The stretched rear swingarm comes from Trac complete with threaded lugs to mount a nitrous bottle. In this case, the crew went with an MPS dry system good for about 40 squirts of the go-juice before refilling. Coolest of all, the bike features a forward-facing exhaust manifold for spent nitrous gasses, making the bike's front end almost appear to snort like an angry bull after a run. Regular gasses are handled via a set of Graves titanium underseat exhausts. When used at the strip—where the McCoys have recorded quarter-mile times in the 8-second bracket—the MPS air-shifter helps throw the cogs on a transmission equipped with race-cut gearing. The McCoy brothers swear the

A trio of McCoy Motorsports custom Yamaha R-1s. The firm doesn't skimp on speed or style.

The business end of a McCoy custom. Galfer wave brake rotors with matching Galfer race-compound pads and braided lines mean stopping is as serious as accelerating.

A McCoy tradition involves chroming the chassis and drivetrain components and then covering the parts with a semitranslucent powdercoating.

passenger pegs were left in place because, despite the high state of tune, this machine is still civil enough to be ridden down to the local Hooters for a show or two.

With several YZF Yamaha customs under their belt, the McCoy brothers have developed a keen eye for what works and what doesn't on a custom sportbike. Check out the way the RC Components Bandit wheels have been polished along the outer rims and the tines powdercoated to match the bike's detail work. Even the fittings on the braided steel hoses and brake lines have been powdercoated to match the bike's theme, the sort of detail that can garner a builder serious points with fans and bike show

Spent nitrous oxide gasses are expelled courtesy of this unique exhaust release valve located between the headlights.

judges alike. Galfer braking rotors, a Hyperpro shock, and Graves engine covers finish a look that says "bling, but business all the way."

A custom sportbike on this level is clearly beyond the capacity of all but the most experienced builders, guys like Mike and Shane McCoy, who have fully equipped machine shops and technicians at their disposal. However, the late model Yamaha R-1 is proving such a popular mount for tuners, the aftermarket is responding with a wide variety of bolt-on components that can turn a stocker into a stunner with even moderate mechanical skills. Many of the signature parts adorning the Arachnophobia bike—like the extended swingarm, wheels, exhaust and nitrous system— are available at most performance shops and, with the help of a skilled technician, can be bolted in place in a few hours. The custom finishes, hand-sewn seats, and special something about a bike like this, however, are another story.

IMITATION OR FLATTERY?

In the custom aftermarket industry for automobiles, car builders and the mainstream manufacturers enjoy a

New York's Dennis Pagalilauan inspired Yamaha with his tasteful 2000 R-1 street and show machine.

This wild, MV Agusta-inspired tail section was sourced from Europe via the Internet.

Pagalilauan saw the potential for underseat exhausts on an R-1 four years before Yamaha.

relationship far cozier than any experienced by custom motorcycle builders. It's a well-known industry secret that each year, all of the major automakers sell a new model of any of their current lineup to the custom houses for $1 each. The practice is intended to encourage the custom shops to create aftermarket goodies for the new rides, which help make the cars more appealing the tuners. If you can't imagine that ever happening between, say, Honda and a back-alley streetfighter shop, that's because it never does. But some builders know that their custom sportbikes have inspired the factories, even if it happens on the down-low.

Take Dennis Pagalilauan's 2001 Yamaha R-1, for example. Every detail on this cherry Champions Edition model is pretty much a unique idea by the New York–based builder or a reworked aftermarket part from Europe. The problem is, Pagalilauan says, after parking the motorcycle outside a watering hole in Daytona, he was shocked to see several Yamaha executives from Japan hovering around his machine, spanning dozens of digital photos, and generally scoping out his work like tigers on a T-bone steak. "They kept complimenting me in what little English they spoke. But it was clear they liked the bike and wanted to study it," he said.

And study it they did. By three model years later, Pagalilauan's jaw dropped when he spotted the latest Yamaha YZF sporting underseat pipes, a more radically upswept tail unit, and other touches frighteningly similar to his. Imitation is something a high-end custom sportbike builder will want to grow accustomed to, and the owner of this blue and white screamer has turned the experience into a positive.

He's since opened his own shop, X Power Motorsports (XPM), in his native New York, focusing his energies on providing full, ground-up builds of R-1s and other 4-cylinder sportbikes. Among the special details XPM works into its machines are the stealthed-out switches for the nitrous bottle that are just barely visible on the left-side intake duct. Though the underseat exhaust unit, which mimics that of a sleek MV Agusta is from BOS, a defunct Dutch aftermarket house, XPM has filled the gap by reworking undertails with built-in exhaust pipes from other suppliers. Pagalilauan hand-builds his own carbon fiber airboxes, which add mad cold airflow to the EXUP-equipped 1,000-cc engine, with the mapping assisted by a Dynojet Power Commander unit.

Nearly all of XPM's machines share this bike's factory-inspired paint job, the owner making no bones about his distaste for murals and other fantasy art. As a result, the machine is factory enough to please the paddock crowd but funky enough for New York. Toss on a generous helping of chrome in the stock rims and frame, and we're talking a 175-horsepower boulevard blaster with the looks to back up the performance.

THE BUILD

Nick Anglada of Florida's Custom Sportbike Concepts (CSC) has spent more time on the custom sportbike show circuit than most of us have on motorcycles. He's seen plenty of mind-bending 'Busas over the years, having taken home his share of trophies for bikes he's built. But when it came time to create a motorcycle that would break all the rules, he turned to another Suzuki model, the racetrack-inspired GSX-R 1000, for inspiration. Said Anglada, "It seems like everywhere you look, people are doing the same things to their Hayabusas. And there are so many aftermarket parts available for those bikes, it really doesn't take the kind of imagination

Nick Anglada's top-shelf custom plan involved chrome plating and then powdercoating his parts in a slick, candy red finish.

The engine's cases were polished after removal, the frame then bolted back in place.

it once did to win a show with one of those bikes. I started by looking for a bike that nobody else was even considering for a show bike and chose the GSX-R 1000."

Anglada appreciated the Suzuki's stubby wheelbase and he saw in its controversial, flat-and-wide tail section an opportunity to show off custom brightwork on a show machine's rear end not readily available to Hayabusa builders. Unfortunately, there was little available in the way of custom bolt-ons for this machine, though Anglada's machine shop and metalworking skills were enough to overcome these problems.

The right side of the engine reveals the matching red wiring that Custom Sportbike Concepts installed for detailing.

This rear shock spring was chromed and powdercoated, though the spring's resiliency becomes somewhat compromised in the process.

A must-have for any serious custom sportbike builder—several extra hands to help lift heavy engine components and assist with complex wiring jobs.

Here, Nick attaches the chromed subframe to the main chassis rails. A delicate, deliberate hand is needed to reassemble finished parts, and Nick says he typically covers all finished areas with shop rags or terrycloth towels before getting anywhere near them with a wrench in hand. One slip or dropped wrench could mean a trip back to the platers.

His main vision for the bike involved unusual finishes and an extrawide rear end. Combined with the Suzuki's short wheelbase, Anglada would end up with a show-winning streetbike with the voluptuous, eye-pleasing dimensions of a young Pamela Anderson. Only less expensive….

Nick started his bling bike project with a barely used, 2005 model Suzuki GSX-R 1000. The machine, as all the best full-on custom bikes are, was stripped down entirely, the individual parts laid out for inspection. With the motorcycle reduced to a manageable pile of parts, Nick

Red rubber tubing was used to cover exposed wiring in the stock wiring harness. Available at most electrical supply stores for a few bucks, the covering provides an excellent way to color-match your bike's electrical circuitry with its theme tones.

Petal-shaped brake rotors from Galfer Braking Products not only look the business, they offer superior cooling over stock brakes.

The Suzuki's front forks were shortened by 2 ½ inches by completely removing the internals, springs, flow valves, and all, then machining the internal fork stops and placing the assemblies back together with shortened springs. Up front, the stock brakes went to the used parts bin in favor of a set of Performance Machine radial calipers, which were also chromed and powdercoated. Braking is handled courtesy a set of Galfer's Wave rotors with braided steel lines.

started selecting which components he'd keep and which would be replaced. For the most part, the GSX-R retained most of its original equipment, the rear end undergoing the majority of the radical modifications.

"A lot of people think they're going to win the big custom shows by chroming everything or building up their bike's motor to some ridiculous proportions. The problem is, nobody can see a big-bore kit or a set of ported heads, so it's the finishes that make all the difference," Nick said. To that end, he shipped off the Suzuki's chassis, forks, and running gear for triple show chrome plating. The subframe rails, shock spring, clip-on handlebars, rotor mounts, and several other parts were then sprayed with a sharp candy red translucent powdercoat after chroming, lending the parts the look of anodized aluminum accessories.

This being an experimental process, the electrostatic powdercoat didn't adhere instantly to some of the chrome parts. The swingarm had to be stripped of its chrome and polished with a buffing wheel before the powdercoat was reapplied.

Here, shop mechanic Adam Chumita ensures proper alignment of the extended swingarm with the shock absorber and rear wheel spindle. The American Metalworks rim runs from power supplied by twin DID gold chains operating via a countershaft visible next to the rear brake rotor.

As the manufacturer and fabricator of an extensive line of custom sportbike parts including wheels, triple clamps, and swingarms, Custom Sportbike Concepts started work

on a single-sided swingarm for the GSX-R. Not only did the new wheel carrier have to be designed from scratch, it would hold a rear rim up to 12 inches in width, accommodating a 330-millimeter Avon Venom rear tire on an American Metalworks rim. The design is based on a similar and highly successful single-sided swingarm that

Above left: The stock fairing support is back from the finishing shop, though builders must be very careful to ensure that all of the stock parts fit seamlessly with whatever aftermarket goods were chosen. With the front end shortened, extra care had to be made during the initial planning stages to ensure that the front fender would not bash into the radiator during aggressive braking. Above right: Among the multileveled brightwork rests tiny details like these custom fluid reservoirs filled with — get this— purple hydraulic fluid! The end caps were treated to the same chrome and powdercoating finish as the frame and other hard parts.

American Metalworks provided this chromed, 12-inch-wide rear rim.

American conceived for the Suzuki Hayabusa; it features full billet aluminum construction, thick 4-inch sidewalls, and fairly easy installation. With 3 inches of extension over the stock arm, the CSC model doesn't compromise cornering the way a 6- or 9-inch extension would.

The engine was left stock by CSC, who favors reliable, easy-to-start-and-maintain engines over extreme horsepower. The stock airbox did receive a free-flowing BMC air fil-ter, and the stock stubby exhaust was replaced by an even shorter Race Fit pipe made from Grade 1 titanium.

Red rubber tubing was used to cover exposed wiring in the stock wiring harness. Available at most electrical supply stores for a few bucks, the covering provides an excellent way to color-match your bike's electrical circuitry with its theme tones.

Off came the factory clutch and stator covers, replaced not by readily available heavy-duty parts from a popular racing supplier, but machined in-house at Custom Sport-bike Concepts. When asked why he preferred to take the tough road in this area of construction, Anglada said he's convinced he could fabricate a part superior to those available from other manufacturers. Naturally, this isn't an option available to your average at-home custom bling-bike builder, but it does reveal the level of dedication and inge-nuity that builders at the top level are willing to invest.

The Suzuki's front forks were shortened by 2½ inches by completely removing the internals, springs, flow valves, and all, and then machining the internal fork stops and placing the assemblies back together with shortened springs. Up front, the stock brakes went to the used parts bin in favor of a set of Performance Machine radial calipers, which were also chromed and powdercoated. Braking is handled cour-tesy a set of Galfer wave rotors with braided steel lines.

The stock fairing support is back from the finishing shop, though the builders must be very careful to ensure that all of the stock parts fit seamlessly with whatever

Here, Adam makes a third measurement of the rear rim, making sure the custom 300-millimeter tire will mount with ease. Most tire-changing machines are too small to handle these monster bike tires.

Chromed and polished small hard parts are expensive, time-consuming, and cool.

Refitting chassis components after a visit to the chrome or powdercoating shop can be a real eye-opener. Or more like port opener if the plater hasn't done a thorough job of securely taping shut all threaded holes before a dip in the vats. Parts can sometimes return from the finishing shop just a hair's-breadth too large to fit comfortably with other parts; to this end, CSC's Adam does a mock-up fit with the subframe and chassis before bolting anything together. Excess materials blocking parts from fitting together must be slowly filed away with great care.

The rear swingarm is machined from a single piece of billet aluminum.

aftermarket goods were chosen. With the front end shortened, extra care had to be taken during the initial planning stages to ensure that the front fender would not bash into the radiator during aggressive braking.

Nestled in the multileveled brightwork rest tiny details like these custom fluid reservoirs filled with—get this— purple hydraulic fluid! The end caps were treated to the same chrome and powdercoating finish as the frame and other hard parts.

Here, Nick attaches the chromed subframe to the main chassis rails. A delicate, deliberate hand is needed to reassemble finished parts, and Nick says he typically covers

Precise measurements are taken to ensure that the swingarm fits safely in the stock mountings. Note the inboard brake rotor.

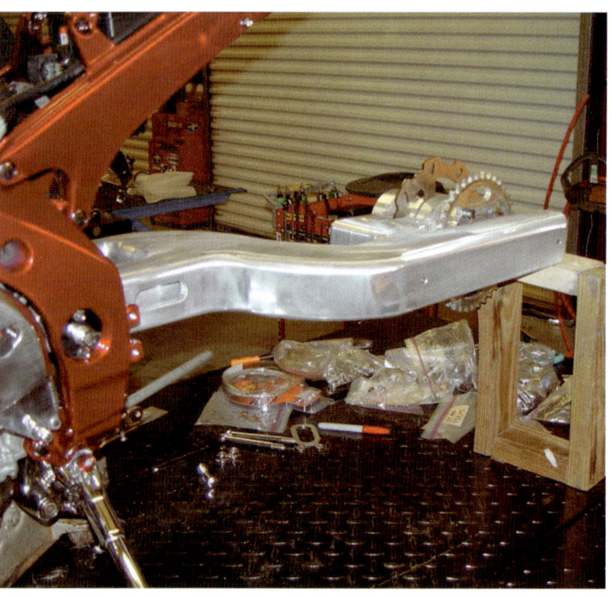

Above left: Though the swingarm will be chromed and powdercoated to match the frame, it's test-fitted in the raw. Above right: A massive 12-inch chrome rear rim is fitted.

all finished areas with shop rags or terrycloth towels before getting anywhere near them with a wrench in hand. One slip or dropped wrench could mean a trip back to the platers.

The LED taillight is test-mounted to the chromed subframe. Mounting rubber or aluminum bushings and washers over all connectors for the electrical components is a no-brainer at this stage. Chromed steel on metal connections can be interesting in a rainstorm if improperly insulated!

Refitting chassis components after a visit to the chrome or powdercoating shop can be a real eye-opener. Or more like port opener, if the plater hasn't done a thorough job of

Above left: Sportbike fans are divided over whether these gargantuan rims are functional, as they slow a motorcycle's steering considerably. Above right: A close-up view of the CSC bike's rear end.

The tire finally mounted, the crew begins final assembly.

securely taping shut all threaded holes before a dip in the vats. Parts can sometimes return from the finishing shop just a hair's-breadth too large to fit comfortably with other parts. To this end, CSC's Adam does a mock-up fit with the subframe and chassis before bolting anything together. Excess material blocking parts from fitting together must be slowly filed away with great care, he said.

This is where function sometimes takes a pillion seat to form in high-end custom sportbike construction; after being both chromed and powdercoated, the stock shock spring will offer little of the damping it was designed to provide. The shock's main coil mechanism was also meticulously polished before reassembly. Nevertheless, with a set of rigid lowering struts in place, the rear end of this

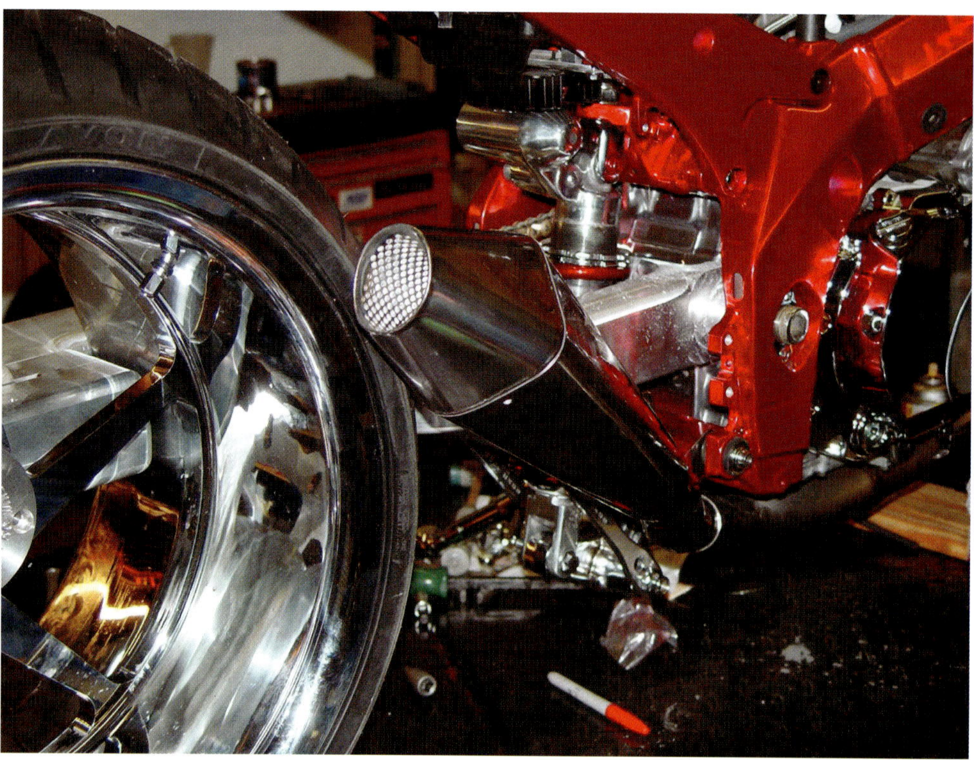

Though many have derided the K5 GSX-R 1000's stubby, MotoGP exhaust, the people at Custom Sportbike Concepts dig it and have worked up a titanium version.

All completed, Custom Sportbike Concepts has transformed the race-replica GSX-R into a serious bling machine.

motorcycle is now intended to be one that looks good and accelerates quickly from a dead stop, not one for the quick cornering as Suzuki designed.

The rear shock retains some of its stock 4½ inches of travel despite being 2 inches lower than it was after leaving the factory. This was handled by bolting on a set of rigid Cus-

tom Sportbike Concepts lowering links. The firm's in-house design department also handled the billet swingarm-mounted license plate mounting bracket, complete with an LED taillight.

In the Suzuki's odd, tortoiseshell-shaped tail section, the stock indicators were removed and Bondo putty used to

Left: This paint job is a multifaceted blend of realistic flames, hard and soft finishes, and geometric shapes.

Below: Coating a tire in Armor-All protectant is great for the show circuit but not advised for the street.

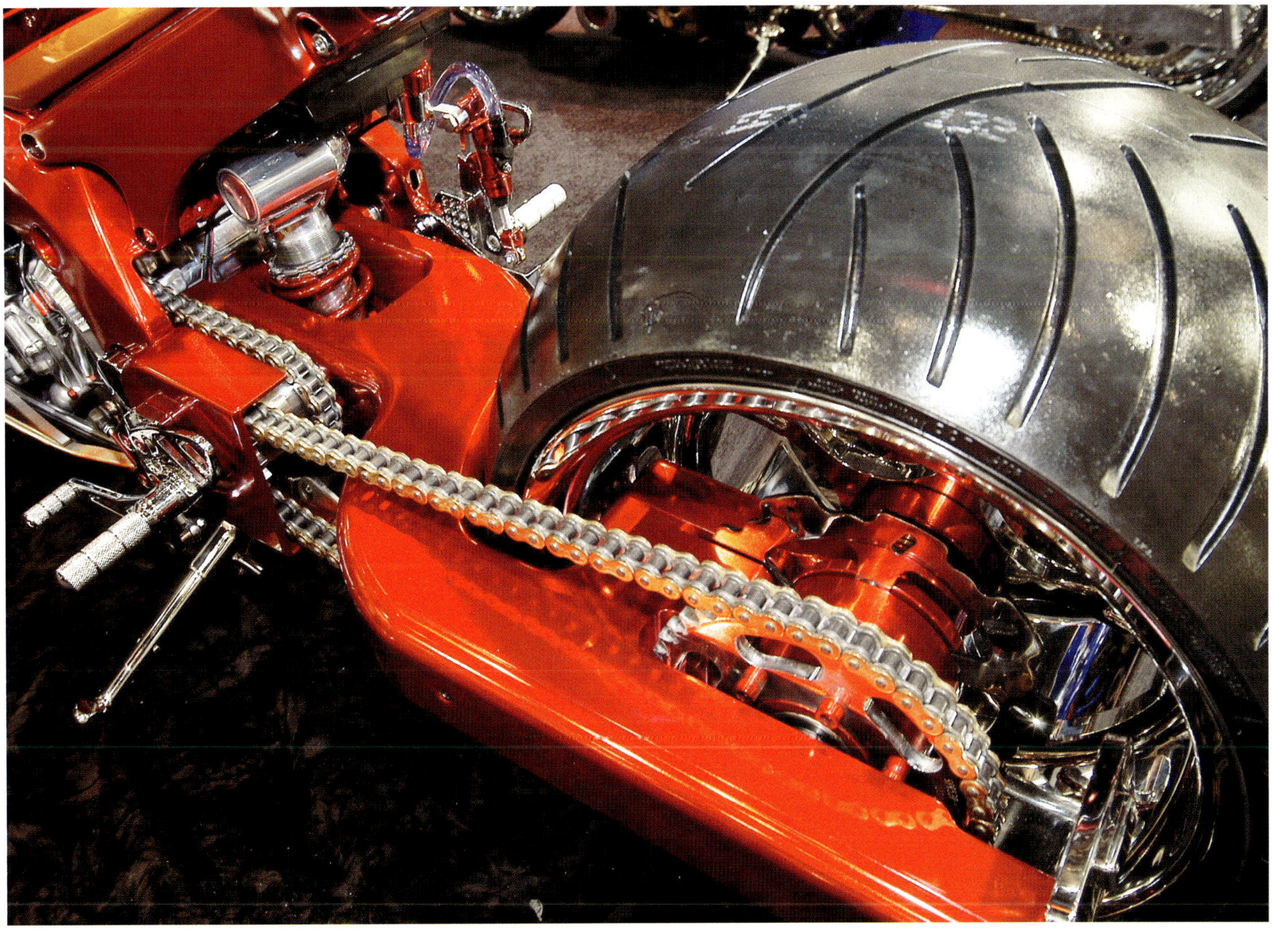

Racing-style adjustable rearsets make all-day rides a breeze, even for the long of leg. Note the extensive chrome detailing throughout the right side of this machine.

smooth over the mounting holes on the Extreme Graphics undertray. Though barely visible—especially with a model smartly planted on the seat—the Suzuki still sports road-legal turn signals, but these are tony LED models molded into the tail section just below the seat. All the bodywork was handled by Todd Fisher from Volusia County Customs, who created the complex paint scheme combining flames along the bellypan and geometric shapes on the fairing uppers and gas tank.

Custom Sportbike Concepts provided the holed, billet aluminum grips that were chromed to match a set of their own hand levers. Each individual fastener was either chrome-plated or polished and powdercoated to match the bike's red base color. Details like this, Anglada said, make all the difference in going home from a bike show with a trophy and going home empty-handed.

A labor of love only a bike show judge could appreciate is the difficult and exacting process of polishing the engine cases. Using a hand-held buffing wheel, the process can absorb dozens of hours as many motorcycle engines must first be stripped of protective, heat-resistant paint before the bare aluminum is exposed. Because clearcoats tend to yellow over time, there's little a custom builder can do to protect polished bare metal, other than strip the machine down and start buffing again. CSC recommends a high-speed buffing tool and a wipe-away buffing compound like Never-Dull for lasting finishes.

The undertail shows the level of bodyworking skills employed. Try finding a seam or line.

Show or go, a bike like this will get you noticed.

RESOURCE GUIDE

Custom Sportbike Concepts
Motorcycle fabrication, wheels, swingarms, paint
(888) 9CHROME
18889CHROME.com

Superbike Concepts
Complete motorcycle builds, custom parts, paint
(772) 219-8529
superbikefl.com

McCoy Motorsports
Race and show motorcycles, custom parts
(606) 432-1556
tobefast.com

Myrtle West Cycle
Custom paint, parts, wheels
(866) 593-3258
myrtlewestcycle.com

CHAPTER 4
BUILDING A STREETFIGHTER: COME OUT SWINGING

My first-ever glimpse of a streetfighter motorcycle came during a visit to Great Britain in the early 1990s. Sitting, like most tourists, in the rear of one of London's fabled black taxis, I noticed an odd-looking motorcycle idling loudly across the crowded intersection. The bike's upside-down front end was topped by a pair of oversized headlights that appeared to have been stolen from a car. The rider's gloved hands clutched a set of what looked like handlebars from a motocross bike, while the exhaust can—or what little remained of it—was burbling like a beehive set on fire.

As the lights changed, the rider noticed himself being stared at and obligingly hoisted a massive sky-high wheelie as he crossed the intersection. As he rode by on one wheel, I noticed the stock plastic bodywork was all but missing from the bike, the gas tank and tiny seat unit painted in an ugly white and gray urban camouflage.

Was this a prop from Mel Gibson's *Road Warrior*? Some poor motorcycle courier who had dropped his machine so many times that he'd refused to replace the damaged fairings? Or had I just witnessed some hip new custom motorcycling movement that us poor old cruiser-obsessed American hadn't heard of?

A few days later when I stopped by a neighborhood newsstand and found a copy of *Streetfighters* magazine, I realized I'd just stumbled across all of these things and more.

Across the pond where the whole stripped-down and badass sportbike trend started, experts say the concept grew out of a love of 4-cylinder Japanese superbikes in the late 1970s. Machines like the Suzuki GS1100 and Yamaha's XS1100 may have had all the aesthetic allure of an aluminum bread box, but the straightline performance they offered was the closest street riders could get to genuine race-track levels of acceleration. Because of the often flimsy tubular steel chassis these early superbikes rode upon, handling, particularly in high speed corners, was frightful enough to have veteran riders questioning their belief in an afterlife.

Just as Italian firm Bimota had done since the 1970s, several small British engineering houses realized that dedicated riders would pay handsomely for a custom-made frame capable of harnessing the awesome power of the

A natural streetfighter right out of the box is Suzuki's TL1000S. Dig the Ducati single-sided swingarm and one-off pipes.

This German Kawasaki ZX-9–based fighter has a radically upturned seat and handmade stubby canister.

Japanese fours. Almost overnight, firms like Spondon, Harris, Martek, and others began filling orders not from professional race teams, but from ordinary backroads junkies looking for an edge on their Sunday morning rides.

Some say it was an accident of engineering that these small-batch chassis turned out to be beautifully crafted pieces of metallurgical art; their swooping, delicately

Spondon's beautifully engineered, sharp-steering streetfighter frames are an industry standard in Europe.

welded frame tubing, their gull-shaped swingarms, and polished surfaces were simply the result of dedicated craftsmen exhibiting pride in their work and a dedication to quality. Whatever the reasons, they looked a damn sight better than any stock motorcycle chassis of the time, and it didn't hurt matters that bespoked frames made for streetbikes could draw attention for their looks as well as their handling prowess.

Not all streetfighter fans were seeking perfect apexes, though. There has long been a love of straightline speed in the European and UK sportbike communities, and when the original chopper craze that swept the United States in the 1970s reached their shores, many Continental riders shunned the idea of building custom cruisers powered by American V-twin motors. Instead, many looked to the ubiquitous Japanese 4-cylinder motorcycle for inspiration, creating low, loud, neochoppers that many say formed the template for the streetfighter scene a few years later.

Instead of painting the new generation of streetbikes to mimic the bikes ridden by favorite superbike racers of the era, their owners borrowed a page from the European chopper scene, enveloping their hand-built screamers with funky, neopsychedelic paint schemes, copious amounts of chrome detailing, and wacky images from beer bottles, comic books, and even pin-up art. They found ways to mount skulls, Simpson motorcycle helmets, and horror masks onto their front forks, routing headlight beams menacingly through the eye sockets. And since not every custom sportbike enthusiast on the European continent could afford to have a custom-made frame delivered to their door, many less affluent riders hopped on board the trend, creating some incredible custom sporting tackle out of factory machines that just happened to have met an unfortunate end on some sharp curve somewhere.

There were few rules to the streetfighter game, only that a motorbike be fast, original, and imbued with an undeni-

Wicked custom built around the remains of a crash-damaged Yamaha Thunderace sportbike with a sports-braced swingarm from EMC and an R 1 tail.

Factory fighters like this Voxan Black Magic continue to push the design envelope.

able sense of cool. If clip-on handlebars gave you a pain in the neck, lop 'em off and bolt on a set of motocross bars, making the bike easier to steer through urban traffic and far easier to wheelie. Seen too many GSX-R 1100s in the local pub parking lot? Strip off your bike's fairing, paint the wheels florescent purple, add a big-bore kit and the minuscule tail section from a Ducati 916.

As with custom choppers back in the United States, the streetfighters (as these bikes were soon dubbed) received plenty of bad press. It didn't help matters that whenever a group of streetfighter riders congregated, impromptu horsepower and wheelie contests broke out. As a result, the bikes were derided as unsafe, antisocial, and a clear indicator that motorcyclists were, indeed, unsavory individuals. Of course, market forces eventually calm any society's nerves about new pop culture trends and the streetfighter was no different. Any bad press these hooligan machines may have received was soon squelched by the sound of a burgeoning parts aftermarket that placed organ pipes, chromed chassis, and a set of Renthal handlebars in the window of every High Street motorcycle dealership.

Always late to a street party, the motorcycle manufacturers themselves waded into the fray in the middle 1990s, offering buyers the first of a long line of factory 'fighters. Triumph's Speed Triple of 1997, with its very deliberately styled twin bug-eye headlights was perhaps the most obvious admission from the corporate world that streetfighters were here to stay. In quick succession, nearly every manufacturer delved into this previously forbidden territory, redubbing them "naked bikes" and offering motorcycles like Aprilia's brilliant Tuono, Suzuki's popular Bandit series,

Buell's sharp-as-nails S-1 Lightnings, Kawasaki's wicked Z-1000, and Cagiva's odd-looking Raptor series.

Some in the sportbike press credit streetfighters as leading something of a backlash against the proliferation of too many serious race-replica streetbikes. They say the onus on riding at or near one's limit on machines like the latest generation supersports 600s, or a liter bike with radial brakes, 180 horsepower, and a race crouch that would give an expert yoga master lumbar pain has turned off many riders. Instead of trying their best to imitate Valentino Rossi on heavily trafficked local roads, naked bike riders have learned how to enjoy life at slightly less than full-bore velocity.

Yamaha's beloved and long-running V-Max has created a unique streetfighter cult all its own.

Instead of worrying if they've achieve proper maximum lean angle when dragging a knee-slider through turns, the streetfighter rider is more concerned with achieving maximum grin factor; smoking the tires for the folks on the sidewalk, and cranking the occasional wheelie for a pretty girl.

To date, the streetfighter has been extremely slow in reaching American sportbike fans, though examples of the style began showing up almost by accident (pardon the pun) on the stunt riding scene early on. Just as many European riders had crafted naked urban machines out of crash-damaged sportbikes, many American freestyle riders simply came to the conclusion that their CBR 900RR would ride better on one wheel with the fairings removed, the clip-ons traded in for a set of tubular bars, and a custom bent exhaust pipe that didn't scrape on the pavement during wheelies.

As a result, most of the streetfighters seen on the road in the United States have lacked the full-on custom treatment bestowed on their foreign cousins. Seldom seen are intricately painted science fiction murals or short, sharp, and madly upswept tail units (a la German fighters). And if there's a Spondon frame available anywhere in America, I've not yet seen it used in anger. Fortunately, a couple of relatively new U.S. shops have entered the streetfighter fray

The Magnum streetfighter, chassis by England's Harris Performance, builders of World Superbike winning frames.

in recent years, offering customers a chance to ride motorcycles possessed of a spirit unlike anything American riders have seen before. On Long Island, New York, A.J. Fulgado's XPO Streetfighter is capturing the no-nonsense style of urban sportbikes for the East Coast market, crafting some stunning examples of the art out of old, air-cooled Suzuki GSX-R 1100s and the occasional Honda CBR 954 RR.

For this chapter's build project we follow Sean Lyons, Irish expat and owner of San Francisco's Streetfighters USA as he builds a wickedly fast, eye-popping classic 'fighter from a Suzuki Bandit 1200. Lyons, a former roadracing protege of Irish racing legend Joey Dunlop, holds several World Records for long-distance and high-speed wheelies. After moving to the United States, Lyons set out to hip American sportbikers to the hottest new trend in

96

Above: Classy Spondon 'fighter from the Isle of Man, complete with Zorstec four-into-two exhaust and Ducati tail section. Below: Rat streetfighters have a style all their own, right down to the aluminum plank seat.

Above: Roadracer Sean Stinnett of Virginia built this quick-steering streetfighter from a stock Suzuki SV650. Stinnett used a GSX-R 1000 tail and an exhaust pipe from a Honda CBR 600RR to make his fighter look as if it came from the factory. Below: Flamethrower-equipped Suzuki Bandit shows why it's not a good idea to tailgate streetfighter riders.

Tom DeTomaso of Cleveland, Ohio, studied European streetfighters long enough to create this stunning, bad and black 'fighter from the remains of a well-used Suzuki GSX-R 750. Big ups for the genuine brass knuckles heel plate, Tom!

performance biking, spreading the streetfighter gospel by building hard-nosed custom motorcycles that are both durable enough for urban streets and handsome enough for the occasional concours show. Lyons admits the streetfighter is a style of motorcycle that's not to everyone's liking. Which is why it's one of our all-time favorites.

CUSTOM CONCEPTS, STREETFIGHTER STYLE: TASTY TLS

Though many dedicated 'fighter enthusiasts insist on using a handmade chassis as the basis for any true streetfighter, British custom builder Mark Barnett's over-the-top Suzuki TL1000S proves this isn't a hard and fast rule. Its motor has been radically reworked with a set of Cosworth high-compression pistons and Yoshimura high-lift cams borrowed from a TL 1000R roadracer. Oversized titanium bellmouths feed the custom-made 60-millimeter injectors, bringing the engine output to an outrageous 145 rear-wheel horsepower.

Mark has even seen fit to replace the standard rotary rear damper with a full Maxton unit bolted to a custom-made tubular aluminum swingarm with a quick-release axle setup made by Martek. The Swedish suspension wizards at Ohlins were responsible for the phat 50-millimeter front end that's custom mounted in a set of one-off, billet aluminum triple clamps from the renowned streetfighter frame makers at Harris.

That's a stock TLS front fairing, but you'd be at pains to find one like this. Barnett, who imports motorcycles from the United States to Europe for a living, had this one custom cut to further expose the brilliantly chromed aluminum trellis frame and a set of gold-plated Renthal handlebars.

The TL provides a popular platform for building streetfighters, beloved for their torquey, twin-cylinder engines and their curvaceous lines, representing what many say was the last motorcycle with an organic look before razor-sharp angular bodywork overtook the industry. Its aluminum trellis frame also adds to the TL's appeal among customizers, as it resembles a far more expensive custom chassis, even in stock form. This one has been blessed with a set of Dymag carbon fiber wheels that weigh less than a set of sturdy rid-

Famous street metal. This Hayabusa naked bike was once owned and ridden by stunt ace Gary Rothwell.

ing boots; while a set of blue-anodized Beringer six-piston racing calipers bring this incredible example of streetfighter art to a halt.

Most of the TL-powered streetfighters we've seen are fairly simple hacksaw jobs, machines that were constructed with lightweight and uncomplicated looks foremost in mind. By simply removing the front fairings and adding a set of tall bars, the TL is an entirely different machine—as evidenced by Cagiva's Raptor, which follows basically the same simple formula. Barnett, of course, took a far different route, one not available to most TL fighter fans, but a level of artistry available to anyone with the time, dedication and, oh yes, did we mention money? In fact, Barnett was not shy about his baby, explaining that he's got over $60,000 tied up between the axles with more changes to come.

A popular bike on the UK show circuit, Barnett's Suzuki reveals what can be achieved when the credit card has a tall limit and the owner has a keen eye for making streetfighters look good while not completely abandoning all of its factory design elements. Beauty, apparently, does not come cheap.

XPO STREETFIGHTER

A.J. Fulgado came into the streetfighter fold after riding sportbikes on the traffic-dense streets of New York City. It's not the type of environment where you could leave a motorcycle with $5,000 rims or a chromed custom-made chassis sitting outside overnight, a reality reflected strongly in Fulgado's vision of what a streetfighter should be. This mean, black, and nasty 'fighter is deep with classic streetbike styling, from its blacked-out treatment of all chrome and brightwork, to its matte black finish that's tough enough to survive an East Coast winter intact.

Fulgado has had a tough road to travel, experimenting with various fabrication techniques over the years because there were no U.S. importers for many of the essential streetfighter components. That means he hand-cut the aluminum for the sleek, upturned undertray mounted to a mock Ducati 916 seat unit that's affixed to a hand-welded subfairing. A set of boffo LED taillights are mated to the custom undertray. Fulgado, who built his first custom bikes solely by looking at photos in a few European custom mags,

Brit custom builder Mark Barnett has created one of the world's most expensive— and beautiful—Suzuki TLS customs, including $3,500 carbon fiber rims.

With the subframe cut and rewelded for a more radical angle, the rear end of this bike is all that and a bag of chrome!

101

even saw fit to track down a unique, dual-headlight unit and a set of DOT-approved handlebar turn signals from German accessory firm Wild Hair.

The set's urban camo covering is also an XPO original, as is the hand-drilled sprocket cover. The engine remains in basically stock condition with the exception of a Dynojet Stage II kit in the Mikuni carbs, a K&N high-flow air filter, and a cleverly crafted, low-level exhaust canister that exits from the custom bellypan just behind the transmission.

"I know Americans love their shiny, blinged-out street-bikes, but I figured with this machine, I'd show them a really different side of the streetfighter phenomenon with something so dark and sinister, it could have just rolled out of *The Road Warrior*," said Fulgado. Despite the motorcycle's hard-edged appearance, there's plenty of painstaking care put into the custom touches, including the completely hidden wiring, tiny green neon detail tubes mounted within the tail section and molding that helps create a sense of flow throughout the bodywork.

FLORIDA 'FIGHTERS

A twentysomething motorcycle painter working on a limited budget, Chris Schuette nevertheless developed a love of funky, stripped-down sportbikes that wouldn't be satisfied. "I knew I didn't have the kind of money it took to bring in a whole boatload of imported parts from Europe, so I sat and stared at my Yamaha R-1 for a long time until I started to get an idea of how I could turn it into a streetfighter just using stuff I had lying around," said the Palm Beach, Florida, native and owner of Pain Inc. Streetfighters.

Though it's difficult to see much evidence of the super-sport Yamaha in the radically customized machine that Chris managed to fabricate, the motorcycle still exhibits the YZF's dangerously quick steering and hyperspeed drive. It took the better part of a year's trial and error in the builder's home garage to perfect the flip-up fiberglass bodywork that characterizes Chris' streetfighters. The units comprise a combination gas tank cover and seat unit, the saddle custom made by the owner, and the rigid, stubby, subframe constructed from the same diamond plate steel used to form semitrailer bumpers. A self-taught bodywork and molding expert, Chris has recently taken to smoothing Bondo over the swingarms and frames of his unique streetfighters, creating a look that's organic and almost startling to see up close.

The engines in his Yamaha-based machines remain mostly stock for the simple reason that Chris believes that

Motocross handlebars top a set of road and track forks from the suspension experts at Ohlins.

Above: New York's A.J. Fulgado's XPO Streetfighter represents the naked bike discipline nicely in the United States. Below: Fulgado's blacked-out and raw Suzuki 'fighter was even featured at a museum show. Custom sportbikes as high art?

Above: Many U.S. stunters came by the streetfighter look by accident after crashing their faired machines. Below: XPO's first effort was this clean, functional custom based on a Honda CBR 929-RR. Opposite: A Yamaha R-1 as conceived by Florida's premier streetfighter craftsman Chris Schuette.

unfaired motorbikes with slightly tall handlebars can become quite a handful at speeds over 140 miles per hour. Instead of focusing his energies on making his bikes faster, Chris has invested hundreds of hours creating uniquely themed bikes; one will resemble a Curtis P-40 Tomahawk fighter plane from World War II, while another is modeled after a lizard from one of Florida's swamplands.

Without access to the often costly parts from Europe, Chris fabricated many of the notable bits on his bikes, utilizing a dual-channel exhaust canister that was inspired by one on a subcompact car, for instance, and fabricating his own V-shaped handlebars from rolled steel stock. The single-sided swingarm on one of the R-1s is taken from a Triumph Daytona, but mounted backward. This required an incredible amount of fabrication, Chris said, but it was affordable.

All of Chris' bikes have been relieved of their front fenders, creating an appearance that wouldn't look out of place on a dirtbike, while most of the chrome and polished aluminum has been blacked out or painted over. He uses Race Tech forks, Akrapovic headers, and extraheavy engine case covers from Race Tech as well. For all his invention, Chris has only spent about $6,000 so far.

BLACK AND BAD

Don't let the horns fool you. The bike resembling Satan's show bike is actually Sean Lyon's daily ride on the streets of San Francisco. The owner of Streetfighters USA built this hardcore UK-style fighter from the remains of a 1992 GSX-R 1100, stealthed out in low-gloss black like the best of the northern 'fighters made in English towns like Blackpool and Manchester.

Sean's secret lies in creating machines that appear as well-worn as any courier's bike, but lurking beneath the unspectacular paint and barbecue-grill primer finishes are some serious performance bikes, known to embarrass riders of far more glitzy iron. Sean's 'fighter runs a 1,216-cc big-bore kit from Wiseco, complete with high-compression pistons. The bottom end has been fully balanced and blueprinted, while the flat slide Mikuni carbs have been rejetted with Dynojet equipment and the stock airbox tossed out rather than just enlarged for additional airflow.

The single-sided swingarm jutting out from behind the stubby chassis is borrowed from a Ducati 748. Sean says mounting the Italian swingarm is a very complicated job requiring very advanced engineering skills. Not only do custom bent exhaust headers have to be fabricated to

Continued on page 109

105

Above: Schuette's custom 'fighters are made entirely of homemade parts of his own design. Below: Color-matched finishes and a swingarm vulcanized from a Triumph Speed Triple, Schuette's customs are the result of lots of talent and plenty of experimentation.

Cleared for takeoff, this machine brings high concepts to the 'fighter game.

Above: Another of Schuette's military-styled machines featuring homemade canister exhaust and flip-top, single-piece tank and tail section.

Right: High-rise, left-side exhaust canister made from hand-welded sections of pipe.

Sean Lyons of San Francisco's Streetfighters USA built this mean-looking street machine.

Continued from page 105

utilize the Ducati rear end, the shock absorber mounts had to be relocated into a set of custom frame mounts. The hand-bent exhaust pipes took the better part of six months to get exactly the draw and length the owner wanted—they're wrapped in a mean black fiberglass heat wrap that the owner says added an extra three horses to the already formidable 190-horsepower top end.

Sean stresses there are easier routes to a similar look for home 'fighter builders. The single-sided swingarms from Honda's VFR Interceptor bolt onto other manufacturer's frames far more easily than the Italian unit he used, and rather than spending months fabricating his own Devil's-head headlight cluster and upswept seat unit, Sean could have simply found comparable items through an Internet search. But that, the builder says, defeats the whole purpose of a streetfighter. "It's supposed to have an artistic element, a style that's all your own. It's supposed to be a bike that you won't see another one of when you're riding."

A committed wheelie fiend, Sean made his own stubby exhaust canister out of parts from a sportbike whose origins are long forgotten. The canister endcap has been cut away as not to scrape the pavement.

Sean hand-wired the tiny DID lights inside the front face mask and also prefit his fiberglass tailpiece together along with a handmade subframe so he wouldn't have to go back and retool anything once the build process got under

Alien-eye exhaust ports and a Ducati single-sided swingarm are just a couple mods to this radical 'fighter.

Following the ideal that streetfighters can be made from anything, Lyons crafted this rare Honda CBX custom.

A monoshock suspension system was adapted to the CBX frame, now sporting a café racer rear end.

Above: Handmade underseat exhausts and a late-model Sportbike suspension system mean this 1980s Kawasaki can run with modern metal. Left: An old school Kawasaki ZX-10 gets the Streetfighters USA treatment.

way. The front forks hail from the stock Gixxer, though he plans to add one from a Honda 954 RR, which is shorter and will run better on the track, where he actually uses this bike to compete against full-on race machines.

On the road, he says the 'fighter is best at the kind of speeds guaranteed to lose a fellow his license, and after all the extensive frame mods—he shortened it 2 inches after removing the airbox, and shortened the rake by two degrees—the bike turns faster than a retreating Frenchman.

The gearbox remains as the folks at Suzuki intended, albeit with the addition of a smaller rear drive sprocket. "With this gearing, it will easily do 96 miles per hour in first gear, and it has a 216-mile per hour top speed. Guys

get so discouraged when they're trying to follow me, because it doesn't look like a motorbike that anybody has put any time or money into. But that's what we do with streetfighters—we make them ride exactly the way we want them to, and it doesn't have to fit anyone else," the owner said.

THE BUILD

Sean Lyons has a unique perspective on why people build streetfighters. As an Irish native who witnessed the movement grow from a small, very contained, cult movement into a worldwide phenomenon, Lyons says nobody builds streetfighters because they're already satisfied with the style and performance of their current motorcycle. "You build

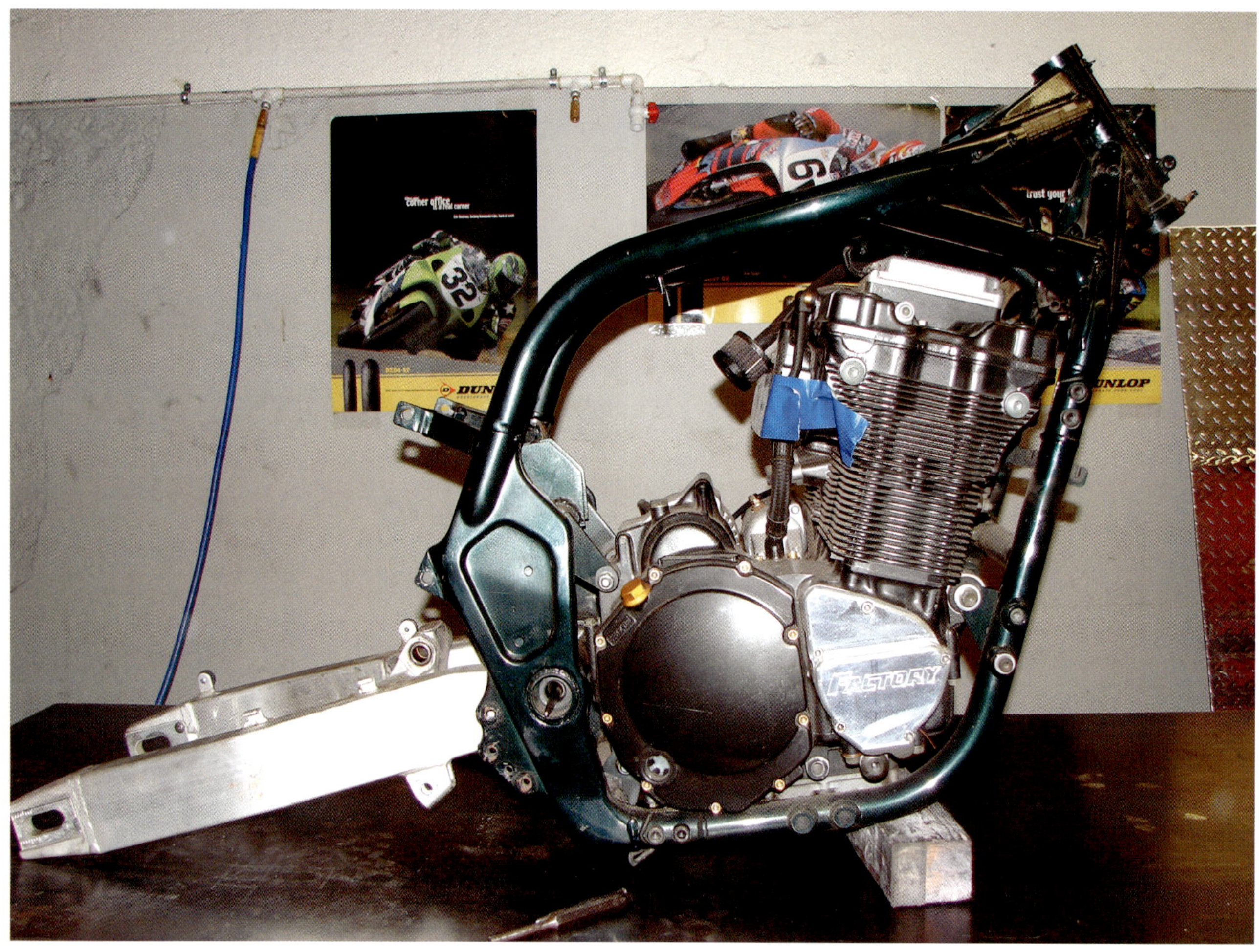

Lyons started with a basic Suzuki Bandit 1200, stripped here for reconstruction.

one of these because you've seen what Suzuki or Triumph can do with a motorcycle and you're just not satisfied. You build a streetfighter because you're convinced that you can do it better on your own terms, using your own parts or your idea of what the perfect streetbike should be like," he said.

With that determination to improve upon factory engineering, Sean started his build project with a nearly stock 1998 Suzuki 1200 Bandit. The big, air- and oil-cooled naked bruiser is perhaps the most popular donor bike for streetfighters in Lyon's native UK, though here in the United States it's hardly engendered that sort of dedicated following. Nevertheless, Lyons can look at a Bandit's sinewy lines and large, exposed engine and see a custom sportbike just begging to emerge.

For starters, Sean stripped the bandit of its stock gas tanks and fenders, sandblasting away the factory black paint and clearcoats. The entire motorcycle was then stripped down to the frame with the intent of spraying the chassis

in a more interesting color, allowing the installation of a single-sided swingarm culled from a Honda VFR 750.

The Bandit's GSX-R 1100–derived engine responds well to some low-buck tuning improvements, this model having had its factory airbox stripped away, to be replaced by a set of paper air filters from K&N. The original clutch cover has also been replaced by a factory racing cover. In these shots, the stock swingarm has already made its slow, sad walk to the dumpster, the VFR rear end standing in place for a mockup build. Note how the inverted front end from a wrecked GSX-R 1000 has already been hung from the fork neck to ensure the new legs will suit the Bandit.

A signature custom earmark for any true streetfighter is a set of wacky, one-of-a-kind headlights. While many builders spend months perfecting headlight clusters involving old motorcycle helmets and human skulls, Sean opted for a mock-up of the famed yellow and black Arai helmet worn by Irish roadracing champ Joey Dunlop. Not crazy enough to actually split a $500 Arai helmet in half for this

Measuring and marking the top triple clamps for the unique headlight bucket.

This sheetmetal support will hold an entire motorcycle helmet and twin headlights when completed.

Lyons's shop contains a complete machine shop service for welding, fabricating, and serious custom work.

A horizontal milling machine is used to fashion a headlight brace from sheet metal.

Advanced skills such as welding can often be farmed out during a more complex streetfighter project.

project, Sean decided to fabricate a replica from a cheaper, throw-away helmet found sitting around the shop.

But before he gets around to the relative fun of decorating his bike with a replica helmet, Sean's crew at Streetfighters USA sets about designing the system of elaborate brackets and mounts needed to support the unique headlight configuration. Here, the team uses a horizontal milling machine to fabricate the top bracket that will hold the twin headlights in place.

Sean uses a piece of marking paper to find where on the forks his mounts will attach to the triple clamps. He can later use the paper as a pattern for cutting out the aluminum bracket parts from stock. One of the keys to creating a memorable streetfighter headlight cluster involves carefully concealing the wiring, which Sean does by routing it through the rear of the helmet and beneath the gas tank.

With a fully equipped machine and fabrication shop at his disposal, Sean has no problem welding the brackets he needs without needing to ship any parts out to subcontractors. A convex-shaped bracket is hand-pounded and then rounded to perfection on an English wheel before being fitted in place atop the handlebar mount. The top triple clamp has been drilled to accept the risers needed to mount a set of gold anodized Renthal tubular handlebars, a must-have for any self-respecting streetfighter fan. Renthal and other firms manufacture their bars hollow, allowing builders to route their wiring internally for a cleaner appearance.

With the brackets welded together and then bolted in place atop the forks, we can see how involved the creation of custom-made mounting hardware really is. Sean, a trained helicopter mechanic, designed the unit to be self-supporting so no weight from the helmet would affect the

Right: Built from "parts found in your average garage," Sean measures to fit a GSX-R subframe to his 'fighter.

Below: The Bandit's subframe is cut with a hand power saw, and the GSX-R unit bolts easily on to the Suzuki fittings.

Left: Measure twice, curse once!

Below: The Bandit streetfighter also received a swingarm from a Honda VFR 750, which bolts on easily to the stock frame mounts.

Right: The spray booth is opened and Sean coats the frame parts in a cool seafoam green.

Opposite top: The gas tank, fenders, and tail unit are sprayed green as well, detailed with a mural of Irish roadracing hero Joey Dunlop.

Opposite bottom: The engine is bolted back in place in the freshly painted chassis.

track of the lighting beams while in use. Ratcheting on the support bolts into the triple clamp pinch bolts, these will receive an extra dose of thread locker to make sure everything stays put on the road.

Look closely at this photo and you'll notice that the Suzuki's top triple clamp is from a TL 1000S twin. It looks as if it's been switched around in a complete 180-degree move, with the ignition switch now in front of the handlebars! This was done, Sean said, to enable use of the triple clamp pinch bolts as mounting points for the custom headlight bracket. It's not unusual to see streetfighters sporting all sorts of wacky, mechanically unorthodox custom features like this, from rearward-facing engines to exhaust systems pointing directly at the pavement—the sky's the limit here!

The lights secured and a set of braided steel brake and clutch lines installed, a shop mechanic test mounts the Joey Dunlop replica lid. A series of small-diameter screws bolted through the rear of the helmet into the hand-shaped aluminum baseplate will keep the helmet in place even when the owner rides like Joey.

With the chassis still mostly bare of electrical wiring and other accessories, Sean begins measuring the frame's crossmembers for a radical reshaping. The streetfighter look is meant to be radical, and this Bandit will be reborn with a GSX-R 750 subframe and tail, which was designed to point toward the sky at a far steeper angle than stock.

Continued on page 123

Gearbox
REMUS
SPORTEXHAUST
SPROCKET SPECIALISTS
EARL'S

NO SMOKING

Above: The carbureted Bandit has its airbox removed and replaced with open paper filters. Below: A complete front end from a 2004 Suzuki GSX-R 1000 is called into duty for its feisty radial brakes.

Above: The completed headlight cluster is test-fitted to the top triple clamp. Below: Sean bolts on a full titanium exhaust system from European pipe makers MIG.

Twin halogen headlights are a streetfighter tradition, just like wheelies and rolling burnouts.

The Joey Dunlop replica helmet has been hollowed out and prepped with fittings to bolt over the headlights.

Looking ready for a blast along the Irish backroads, Streetfighters USA's Joey Tribute Bike.

Continued from page 118

The frame braces are prepared for removal with a plasma cutter, while the GSX-R subframe is measured to ensure it will bolt into place with the stock Bandit mounts. Sean's 'fighter will sport a fairly conservative seat lift, though many modern streetfighters, particularly those built in Germany and France, sport custom tail units designed to ride almost perpendicular to the ground.

The chassis is stripped bare again and rolled into the shop's spray booth. An unusual choice is this seafoam green, but Sean says it's the perfect match for a streetfighter that will feature a mural of an Irish road scene with Joey riding through the countryside.

Keeping the spray gun about a foot away from the primered and wet-sanded chassis, Sean lays down one coat, waits a few minutes for the Imron paint to dry, and then resprays in short bursts to prevent streaks of drips. Custom painting is an exact science and takes years to perfect. Sean suggests starting out with simple colors like gloss black and teaching yourself sanding techniques before tackling more involved paint schemes.

A look at the completed bodywork, including gas tank, fenders, and undertray. Sean maps out the overall design for his 'fighters before beginning any construction, to ensure that the final, completed motorcycle remains true to his customer's vision.

With the frame painted, the Honda VFR swingarm is mounted to the frame's left side. The single-sided swingarm requires a builder to simply file away a bit of extruded metal on the frame, using the bearings and cup from the VFR in place of the standard Suzuki parts. The stock Suzuki shock

The upturned tail section is pure Euro-fighter, but made from stock Suzuki components.

Lyons and his custom creation ready to hit the road.

absorber requires no modifications to adopt the new swingarm, though a stock Bandit shock would have bolted right into place. This unit is from a Honda CBR 1100XXX Blackbird, which is an improved choice for a heavier bike and rider, the builder says.

The bodywork back in place and the stainless steel pipes polished to a high gloss, the Joey Dunlop streetfighter looks ready to take on any comers at a wheelie contest or a rip along the Isle of Man. Sean of Streetfighters USA says he chose to use so many stock Suzuki components for this project to show prospective builders how easy it is to create a unique custom sportbike using just the parts available at your average bike shop.

"Besides the Joey helmet, most of this is stuff any decent mechanic could build himself in an at-home garage," he said. Notice the way the GSX-R 750 rear end dovetails nicely with the Bandit gas tank, and how the high-rise MI exhaust pipe flows perfectly along the curves of the tail section.

RESOURCE GUIDE

Streetfighters USA
Motorcycle fabrication, machine shop services, parts
(415) 495-0660
streetfighters-usa.com

XPO Streetfighter
Custom motorcycle fabrication
(516) 742-2424
xpostreetfighter.com

Special Edition Motorsports
Spondon frame kits
(310) 364-0255

CHAPTER 5
BUILDING A STUNTBIKE: A CRASH COURSE

Of all the different types of customized sportbikes on the roads, stunt machines are perhaps the most misunderstood. Many novice stunters make split-second decisions about whether or not to embrace the sport, so they end up using whatever motorcycle they happen to own at the time in their pursuits. Salespeople from motorcycle dealerships from across the country will attest to selling brand-new motorcycles to riders who announce that their only intention is to learn to stunt as well as pros like Darius Khashabi or Jason Britton. While these are noble aspirations no doubt, the truth is, many of these same low-mileage machines turn up in salvage yards or in the "Cheap Used Bikes" section of many showroom floors because the owners chose to ride them in stock form.

Despite the unbeatable durability of modern supersports machines, they simply aren't engineered to have their front ends slammed repeatedly to the pavement at high speed after block-long power wheelies. Today's gas-charged shock absorbers offer suspension levels that Grand Prix racers of the 1980s only dreamt of, but their mounting points can't take many stoppies without snapping like twigs. And good luck to the young baller who looks for a "12 o'clock" setting on his bike's rear preload adjuster. And there's a reason for those goofy, fur- or decal-covered fairings and windshields seen on so many professional stunters machines; they help deflect the inevitable crash damage that comes from learning how to get stunts wrong (which any of the pros will tell you is a major part of learning to get stunts right!).

Gonna build a stuntbike? Better load up on zip-ties!

Covering a stuntbike in fake fur is somewhat outdated, but it does protect a bike from the pavement.

With that in mind, customizing a stuntbike can be done to make it look better, run faster, or turn heads just like any other type of personalized ride. The main difference is this: Unlike chromed-out bling bikes, you can stunt faster, farther, and longer by taking the time to make a few changes to your machine. Oh yeah, and taking the proper precautions will actually save you money. "Crash bars and engine cages," stunt legend Wink 1100 used to say, "are cheaper than fiberglass."

Anyone entering the stunt game at this point in history has a far smoother road to traverse than riders did just five years back. The veteran teams have spent a Brinks truck on replacing damaged bike parts, and I specifically recall shooting photos for my book *Streetbike Extreme* back in 2002 and watching Jon-Jon from New York's Wheelie Boyz dump it over the handlebars while rolling an endo. His clutch cover busted and the engine oozing 50-weight, his ride was finished until bike shops opened the following Monday.

That wouldn't happen today. Some of the more inventive freestyle riders got tired of paying for new parts, so they started fabricating engine cages to protect their bike's more delicate bits from the ravages of the road. They bolt on tough magnesium or billet aluminum clutch and stator covers and protective frame sliders designed for the rigors of roadracing, which allows them to drop their bikes practically without a care. This means a visit to the pages of magazines like Britain's *Streetfighters* is equivalent to visiting a freestyle rid-

ers' mall, complete with firms offering everything from replacement fiberglass and plastic bodywork to engine cages and tires designed specifically for hard street riding.

Many stunt riders have started adopting cheap, pliable, aftermarket bodywork kits to their street machines. Designed and supplied by leading roadrace bodywork firms like Hotbodies Racing, these kits can absorb an impact with the pavement and retain their shape in ways that more brittle stock plastic simply can not. With an increasing number of freestyle riders deciding to take their sport off the road and onto the drag strips, running race plastic is an even smarter option because riders can do away with their stock lighting equipment, which always seems to get in the way during a mishap.

Aftermarket bodywork offers other advantages to the stunt riders as well, explains freestyle rider and bike builder Blake Connor. "They don't have inner fairings and they only get in the way when you're trying to ride a 12 o'clock wheelie anyhow. So a race kit eliminates the need to cut your fairing cowl away, and that makes it easier to look at the road ahead past the front wheel when you're riding," he said.

Other professional freestylers, like Tony D. from New Jersey, have taken preparations to their stuntbikes to a level equal to that preferred by top European freestylers; he's created a full-on custom streetfighter for stunt riding, equipped with an elaborate system of frame braces, fork clamps for added stability, and motocross-style tubular han-

With street freestyle riding gaining popularity, sprocket manufacturers like Vortex have begun offering sprockets in amazing sizes for additional torque.

With frequent contact between bike and pavement, repairs are a way of life for a stuntbike.

Professional freestyle rider Jason Britton's ride backs up his claim that a clean, customized stuntbike makes for an impressive performance.

dlebars for added low-speed control. Tony D., one of the few U.S. stunt riders to compete against massively talented Europeans like Germany's Christian Pfeiffer, has picked up on a number of the Euro riders' radical custom modifications and adapted them to his CBR 900RR Honda. There's a fully operational thumb brake mounted on the handlebars for slowing the machine while his feet are busy balancing on the footpegs, and his rear sprocket boasts around 140 teeth and is the size of an old 12-inch record album; as a result, the clutch is seldom needed for cranking the front end and the thumb brake makes relatively easy work of stunts like one-sided flamingoes and stand-up no-handers.

Popular Internet sites like Stuntlife.com and others provide an increasingly broad source of parts for the up-and-coming stunt enthusiast, filling a void where only a few years ago, most riders were forced to make their own parts from scratch.

Reinforcing shock mounts with additional welding is not uncommon for stunters looking to avoid frame and linkage damage, and installing a set of rising rate fork springs from the like of Ohlins or Race Tech is an affordable (most kits sell for under $100) way to beef up your tired front end before it washes out at the wrong moment.

Blown fork seals are a constant source of trouble for hard-riding freestyle riders, the pressures of landing a 500-

pound motorcycle on the front wheel for long periods of time steadily taking its toll. Unfortunately, short of learning how to install replacement seals yourself, there's not much riders can do to reinforce their front ends against leaking seals. The new generation of flush-mount turn signals from the likes of McCoy Motorsports and Lockhart Phillips have done wonders to help prevent roadways and drag strips from being covered in shattered plastic, and many stunters have learned the hard way to relocate their rear indicators inside their taillight modules for an even cleaner appearance.

Dozens of stunt riders we've spoken with are dead set on improving their braking systems, easily done with racing-compound brake pads and a set of braided steel or Kevlar lines. Either of these options vastly improves stopping power—which is not something to take lightly with 500 pounds of sportbike hanging over your head during a rolling endo! To this effect, steering dampers from the likes of Scotts or Hyperpro can also help control a motorcycle riding on one wheel, whether while landing an endo or controlling a tank-slapper after a badly landed wheelie.

Of course, ratted-out stuntbikes are still in effect at events like the annual Starboyz Stunt Fest in Ohio, beloved for their affordability and ease of use. These machines are often the ones we see winning the six-gear burnout contests, because what's the big deal if you gum up the rear end of a 10-year-old, $1,200 bike with a few pounds of burnt rubber? Rat freestyle bikes have the ability to be dropped with no worries about damaging their finish—an approach to the sport that goes a long way toward taking chances and learning the ropes.

But for our money, investing a little time and money to learn the options available for your freestyle machine makes for a safer ride and a bike that will be cranking tail-draggers for a lot longer and a lot farther than the competition. "You show up to do a show on a clean, chromed-out, well-taken-care-of motorcycle and everybody knows that you're a professional, somebody who cares about the sport. Some stunters will say it's too much hassle to keep a bike clean and to constantly be replacing parts when they get damaged, but in my opinion, it's worth it," explained professional stunt rider Jason Britton.

Riders of his caliber, who never fail to arrive at competitions riding perfectly turned-out bikes, will even paint several fairings and bodywork panels in their team's motif in case one gets damaged during a performance. Most pro

Recent trends shy away from rat stunt machines and more toward bikes identified by team colors.

Stunt master "Crazy" Dan Jackson shows why it's important to perform a complete preride check of nuts, bolts, and brakes before a stunt show.

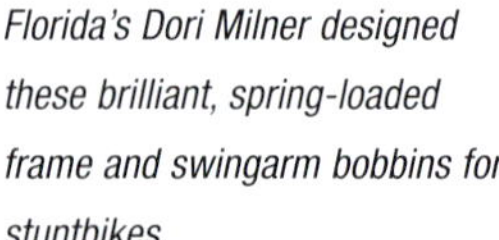

Florida's Dori Milner designed these brilliant, spring-loaded frame and swingarm bobbins for stuntbikes.

Stunt team Freestyle Ingenuity devised this X-shaped engine cage in 2003, to much acclaim.

riders have also invested the time to learn the basics of plastic welding and repair to save cash when things go wrong.

WHICH BIKE'S BEST?

The question of which sportbikes make for the maddest stunt machines is a subject that will have stunters up arguing until the wee hours. While it would seem natural that many would choose twin-cylinder machines for their brutal torque, most American freestyle riders can be seen riding 4-cylinder machines from a variety of manufacturers. Patrick from Sportbike Hype stunt team swears by the Honda CBR 929 RR, a mount popular because the oil pick-up is located at the rear of the engine, which means the motor won't starve itself of fluids during extended wheelies of 1 mile or more. The 929 also benefited from excellent balance and a fairing without an inner-stay, a cumbersome piece of steel that was a chronic problem for riders doing high-chairs and other gas-tank and seat-mounted stunts on older bikes.

Despite being out of production for several years, the 929's predecessor, the venerable CBR 900RR, is still present on the stunt scene, favored for its unbreakable durability, a dense backlog of parts, and the fact that 1994–1998 models balance well, have the power to wheelie without using the clutch, and are dirt cheap.

Older generation 600-cc sportbikes are widely believed to be great for beginners, but the peaky powerbands prevented the middleweights from being used extensively by freestyle riders. "The old 600s were great if you were learning to do stoppies, because they were so light, you shift your weight forward and the back end just floats up into the air," explained Starboy Scott Caraboolad. "Until Kawasaki came

133

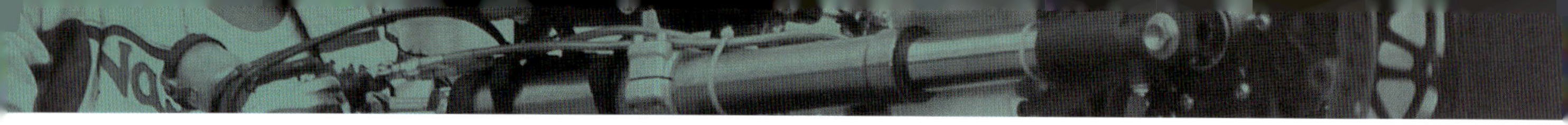

Above: Stunt rider Chauncey Viera shows why shortening an exhaust canister is such a good idea for expert level riders.

Right: Freestyle Ingenuity's frame sliders after one crash-landing prove how well they work!

Opposite: Before discovering the joys of aftermarket replacement fairings, Blake Connor covered his CBR 600 stuntbike with masking tape for protection.

out with the ZX636 a couple of years ago, there wasn't a 600 with the torque and power, not to mention balance, that really worked for all kinds of tough stunts like slow, circle wheelies and fast stuff like switchbacks."

Italian bikes with their fragile electrical systems and high maintenance costs are virtually unknown in the stunt world, with the possible exception of a Ducati S4 Monster ridden by German stunt ace Christian Pfeiffer.

Starboy Dave Sonsky rode an Aprilia RSV Mille for two years and found the big twin well-balanced and blessed with more than enough bottom-end power. But considering the relative expense of the Aprilia, it only made sense to stunt on a far cheaper Japanese-made motorcycle.

STARBOY KEVIN'S BIKE

Though many a stunter favors the easily accessible torque of a twin cylinder sportbike for stunting, many pros prefer the high-revving engines of 4-cylinder liter bikes for their trade. Starboyz founding member Kevin Marino has come a long way in the development of his stunt machines, starting his career on a series of what could be described as the most ill-abused motorcycles on the planet. During a ride with the team during the filming of their FTP III video, a spark plus vibrated out of the socket on Kevin's Honda CBR 900RR, and spongy fork springs left the battered machine with a front wheel sporting several flat spots.

Over the years, the team has learned to refine their bikes to ensure long-term usability. The Honda CBR 954 RR Kevin currently rides was donated by sponsor North American Warhorse, and was immediately torn down in the team's workshop to make it stunt-ready. Among the more notable changes was a Freestyle Ingenuity protective engine cage. This brace mounts in minutes to the Honda's motor mount points, circling the fragile clutch and stator covers with a brace of cold rolled steel.

The brace has proven helpful in other ways as well—one of Kevin's signature stunts is the "chainsaw burnout," which involves tossing the bike over on its side, standing on the swingarm and faring, while whipping the throttle open until the prone motorcycle spins on a tiny contact patch of the rear tire. The Ingenuity brace includes an integral, hardened plastic frame slider that works to balance the motorcycle's bodywork off the pavement during a chainsaw burnout, just as it does during a crash. The advent of these well-built protective braces is a primary reason why stunt riders stopped decorating their rides in fake fur and other protective coverings a few years ago.

Avoiding crashes, or at least the damage sustained by a motorcycle during a get-off, is a major concern for stunt riders, which is why many proponents of the sport opt to

Continued on page 141

Opposite: Starboy Kevin Marino shows mad skillz with a one-handed wheelie, helped by the well-balanced Honda CBR 954RR. Above: A full engine cage courtesy California's Racing 905. Foam padding on the windshield for high-chair wheelies and low tire pressure make this machine work for a pro.

A shortened exhaust can help avoid scrapes and potential tip-overs during 12 o'clock wheelies and can be made easily with a saw and pop-rivets.

The reason stunt riders use protective engine cages.

Freestyle ace Tony D. balancing on his bike's scrape bar in a slow circle wheelie.

Continued from page 135

shorten their exhaust canisters. As full-vert 12 o'clock wheelies became the norm a few years back, riders noticed their stock canisters scraping the ground and occasionally pancaking into the pavement, causing bikes to lose control. Early shortened cans were created by simply hacksawing the mufflers in half and letting the noise and fumes rage from the remains. The Starboyz were among the first stunt teams to bother riveting the end caps to their shortened exhaust cans, creating a cleaner look and quieter sound.

The modification can be completed in minutes, using a band saw, a rivet gun, and heat-resistant glue, though it's advised to ensure that your exhaust can does not taper from one end to the other, which would make refitting the end cap impossible. General prep work for a stuntbike involves applying a thread sealant like Loctite to all the major nuts and bolts. Kevin's Honda has had its mirrors, license plate bracket, and turn signals removed, and he's attached a thick foam rubber pad to the top of his windshield, to prevent cracking when he sits atop the gas tank for "high chair" wheelies.

The stoved-in gas tank is another popular stunter modification that used to come about almost by accident. After a few dozen tank-seated burnouts and wheelies, even the strongest steel gas tanks tended to develop a concave shape. Today, many riders will remove their gas tanks before they begin stunting a new bike, carefully hammering in a shape suited for seating, rather than letting it happen naturally.

Finally, Kev's Honda has the prerequisite oversized rear drive sprocket, this one a massive 80-tooth aluminum unit from Thrust Company. Next to a perfectly developed sense of balance, radically altered gearing is perhaps the surest means of perfecting smooth, clutchless wheelies, the pros say.

TONY D.

Few active stunters on the U.S. scene have invested the sort of time and engineering in their machines as has Tony D., a New Jersey professional freestyle rider. A trained mechanic who got his start with the Mirror Image Stunt Team a few years back, Tony D. has spent a great deal of time training and riding with European stunt riding legends like A.C. Farias, a showman who treats his freestyle machines with all the care and technical know-how bestowed on a championship Tour De France bicycle.

"A lot of riders will just take off a couple of parts from a stock streetbike and try stunting on it, but these same dudes end up crashing out or damaging their bikes so bad, they have to quit riding because the frame's cracked or they broke the fork seals every time they pulled one up," said Tony.

To make sure he doesn't end up an also-ran, Tony decked out the chassis of his barely recognizable Honda CBR

The streetfighter headlight cluster and Renthal motocross bars on Tony D.'s stunt machine.

Above: Intensity and a well-prepared machine has helped Tony D. get his props on three continents.

Right: Twin Nissin brake calipers help control skids on Tony D.'s machine. The devil canister has been radically shortened.

Scrapes and battle damage on the Freestyle Ingenuity cage. Note the homemade mount welded to the frame.

A sprocket the size of an old 12-inch LP makes for easy rear-wheel launches.

900RR with a half-dozen steel braces, welded in place at points where stuntbike frames often suffer damage. There's no exact science to reinforcing a sportbike chassis in this way, and most practitioners will tell you their decisions concerning just where to mount a brace and how thick the steel should be is all a matter of personal preference. Tony's machine is reinforced at the mounting points for his aftermarket Showa shock absorber—a point where stoppies can wreak havoc on frame castings—and at the juncture of the frame and rear subframe. There's a Racing 905 engine cage bolted to the front motor mounts protecting the clutch and stator cover, while the seat unit is braced with a homemade

Continued on page 147

143

Team X-Treem's Buell mounts have few modifications save for scrape bars and talented riders.

New Jersey's Underground Riders have perfected the art of masking their bodywork in team stickers to ward off scrapes and crash damage.

Brian "CBO" Rodine of Des Moines Extremes shows why stuntbikes enjoy such brief lives.

A crashed 2004 Honda CBR 600RR is targeted for a stuntbike project.

Continued from page 143

scrape bar that Tony fabricated himself. A set of street-fighter-style Renthal motocross handlebars are set in a drilled Honda triple clamp, the imported Devil aluminum exhaust canister shortened a good 12 inches for scrape-free wheelies.

Tony engineered his own thumb-operated brake lever, which leaves his feet free from braking duties during those extremely difficult slow circle wheelies. The lever is identical to those utilized by superbike racers and mounts to the left handlebar just below the clutch lever. With his feet free, Tony's riding style centers around balancing himself on the bike's scrape bar and passenger pegs, which are rare accessories to see on a full-on stuntbike.

Up front, Tony mounted a streetfighter headlight visor, deploying two tiny halogen bulbs that are far less likely to shatter during an endo gone wrong. Stiffened fork springs, braided-steel brake lines, safety-wired handgrips, and low air pressure in the tires are all precautions that make this stuntbike one that will likely be on the circuit long after the competition is rusting in the salvage yard.

TEAM X-TREEM

Team X-Treem leader Todd Colbert started his career stunting on a streetfightered Suzuki GSX-R 1100, done up in a style similar to the bike ridden by Welsh stunter Gary Rothwell.

A fiercely talented rider who thrives on displays of sheer horsepower, Colbert surprised his competitors when his team switched brands and began riding a trio of Buell XB 12R Lightnings for the 2003 season. A hard-working team that performs at over 100 shows each year, Team X-Treem chose the Buell lineup because these lightweight, durable, Harley-Davidson-powered bikes require little in the way of major modifications for stunt riding and very little maintenance.

Since receiving the bikes new, Colbert's crew have added bolt-on 12 o'clock bars from Powers Stuntworx to the rear subframe of each of the 1,200-cc machines, and little more. Aftermarket brake pads and hard-wearing Dunlop D207 sport-touring tires are about the only changes. The Buells deploy a rubber/Kevlar belt drive, so altering the sprockets for extra torque is not an option, Colbert explained, though this is seldom an issue for motorcycles with steep lower-end powerbands. The Buell's single perimeter-mounted front brake also makes for excellent endos, requiring no modifications for freestyle action.

For a gas-and-go stuntbike option, it's tough to beat these affordable little twins, though the narrow powerband may not be to everyone's liking.

THE BUILDER

Perfectly illustrating our previously stated point about the relative ease of transforming an ordinary streetbike into a wheelie-crushing, tire-burning stuntbike is our build session with amateur stunter Blake "The Cop Hunter" Kelly. The producer of a popular and hilarious underground stunt video involving instigated squad car chases, third-gear burnouts through crowded supermarkets, and lots of stand-up wheelies, Kelly is a big fan of the Honda CBR 600RR series, a bike he says has the perfect combination of light weight and top-end power for stunt riding.

Kelly had recently suffered a midcorner mishap aboard his own mount, a year 2004 model CBR 600. Rather than repaint the machine's scratched and dented bodywork, he chose to run a set of race bodywork from Sharkskinz. Famous for their ability to withstand repeated contact with asphalt, these race-day fairings and body panels are a simple bolt-on job that attach directly to a sportbike's stock fairing hangers. Kelly had ridden freestyle on the streets for several years, using only several layers of packing tape for protection on his bike's fairings and side panels. Lesson learned, he decided that this new machine would be engineered to withstand anything—well, almost anything—that the forces of nature, concrete, and the law could throw his way

THE BUILD

First, after staring at the wrecked CBR in horror for several minutes, the owner calms himself, thinking of the future, one in which he'll have far fewer headaches while stunt riding a machine actually built in preparation of mishaps. Many novice stunt riders will be satisfied to practice their craft on motorcycles in much worse shape than this low-mileage CBR 600, though it's a known fact that changing a few vital bits will make all the difference in how long the bike remains in running condition. Anyhow, black motorcycles are, like, so passé. . . .

The Honda's stock seat is removed, giving access to the short 12-millimeter Phillips head screws holding the tail section in place. The tail section should lift right out, back and away from the motorcycle, with a minimum of effort. Likewise, the damaged fairings are pulled from the

Builder Blake Kelly removes the damaged stock bodywork from the Honda.

machine, to be stored in safekeeping should the riders ever hope to sell this, um, barely run, nearly pristine motorcycle on the used market.

Wasting little time, our anxious stunt rider lines up a custom-made 12 o'clock bar made by California's Racing 905. The piece is welded from sturdy ¼-inch steel and is available for most late-model sportbikes. The rear bash plate is bolted on to the main structure, allowing riders to replace the unit in parts of it becomes damaged. Notice the slightly angled skid plate that helps assist the motorcycle while rolling along vertically—homemade scrape bar builders often overlook this little lesson in geometry and

end up crafting skid plates that jar the motorcycle dangerously off balance the first time it touches pavement.

Blake lines up the scrape bar's predrilled holes with a set of threaded lugs welded to the subframe. The stock bolts should be replaced by hardened fasteners, which are far less likely to snap while the weight of a 400-pound motorcycle and a 200-pound rider rest on their shoulders. Blake also applies a healthy coating of Loctite to the threads, further ensuring that these important bolts stay in place.

With many of today's popular sportbikes featuring four-into-one underseat exhaust canisters, make sure that any aftermarket scrape bar clears the tailpipe and leaves enough room between the scrape plate and exhaust port for the gasses to escape. While many riders will shorten the exhaust

Right: A scrape bar from Racing 950 will help only if you have the skills to actually use it!

Below: The bar comes complete with a replaceable steel end plate. It bolts directly to most sportbikes with no mods.

canister when encountering this problem, this can have a negative effect on an electronic fuel injection system's mapping. For a few extra bucks, Racing 905 will custom cut a scrape bar that's a few inches longer than necessary to accommodate underseat exhausts.

The owner has already swapped the stock 42-tooth rear drive sprocket for one with two fewer teeth, a modification he says will offer better acceleration at low rpm. The Lockhart Phillips turn signals have also been mounted vertically, with new mounting holes drilled into the subframe just below the taillight. This doesn't exactly offer any advantages while stunt riding, but it sure does look cool!

Likewise, the use of plastic zip-ties on the Sharkskinz tail section is a stylistic, rather than performance, modification. Veteran freestyle riders swear by these babies, which, along with a roll of duct tape, are said to possess the magical powers to fix anything this side of a blown cylinder head.

Though not at all recommended for safety reasons, this is one stunt rider's novel "solution" to a scrape bar blocking the view of his taillight. Blake swears the light is firmly secured with electrical tape and won't fall off when he's busy trying to scrape his front fender on the pavement. The license plate has been relocated to a spot on the underside of the tail section just above the top shock absorber linkage. This is a popular modification for outlaw stunters, but we'd advise otherwise unless you're the type of rider who likes being pulled over by the police. As an alternative, we'd suggest trying a custom side-mount taillight and license plate holder from the likes of McCoy Motorsports if you

Blake test-bolts the bar into place using the factory hardware before installing the Sharkskinz replacement bodywork.

encounter this problem after mounting a scrape bar to your custom stuntbike.

The Sharkskinz street or race bodywork (full street kit, $780) is made of a softer, far more flexible, plastic compound than the brittle plastic used to manufacture stock motorcycle parts. Therefore, Blake found it relatively easy to cut a pair of horizontal slots into his tail section to make room for the Racing 905 scrape bar (about $125 retail) using just a utility knife. Similar alterations to the after market bodywork were also made in the side panels to make room for the protruding engine guard.

The Sharkskinz street bodywork kit comes complete with a nifty gas tank cover that attaches to the frame in minutes requiring few, if any, alterations. Blake used an Allen

151

Using Loctite thread adhesive will ensure no nasty surprises when the bike is vertical.

wrench to remove the hex-head bolts holding the Honda's locking gas cap in place, and on it went. The tail section is predrilled and mounts into the stock bodywork's fittings using original hardware.

Racing 905's Engine Armor guards ($250) are revolutionary in the way they're designed to work as a separate frame member. The apparatus bolts into the motor mounts on either side of the engine, with a main strengthening bar mounted laterally across the crankcases. Using the stock 14-millimeter motor mount bolts, the cage can be mounted easily, after carefully threading the crossbar behind the exhaust headers. Not all aftermarket exhausts will prove compatible with protective engine cages, so check with your supplier and cross-reference before splashing out the bucks.

Everything secured and bolted into place, Blake runs the engine for a few minutes and then lets everything cool

Continued on page 156

Left: The Racing 905 engine cage bolts to the engine mount bolts and is secured by a hardened steel crossbar.

Below: D-shaped and protruding from the engine a good 4 inches, the cage will ensure the fairings never touch the pavement.

BUILDING A STUNTBIKE: A CRASH COURSE

Finished in an easy-to-clean flat olive green, this machine is ready to stunt, whatever the weather.

The first protective engine cages were fabricated by motorcycle messengers in Europe.

Make sure your scrape bar of choice clears the underseat exhaust, or there could be fueling problems.

Another clever use of the ubiquitous zip-tie in repairing damaged plastic.

Continued from page 152

down before rechecking all his fasteners. With the considerable wallop a motorcycle sustains while being chucked down on the pavement after a stunt ride, it's a good idea to keep the wrenches handy and retrace your steps after the first ride, tightening any nuts or bolts that may have worked themselves loose.

A little known fact about the 12 o'clock bar: It makes a handy kickstand, allowing a stuntbike to fit easily into a parking space designed for a skateboard! Keep in mind that motorcycle engines were not designed to operate at such steep angles. Therefore, after standing your stunt machine up for any extended period of time on the scrape bar—while moving or stationary—remember to let the bike rest in a level position for a few minutes to ensure that oil is flowing to all vital areas of the engine.

Another unexpected advantage to running a Racing 905 Engine Armor kit: Chainsaw burnouts can be pulled full-throttle with no worries about scratching or denting your bodywork, frame, or other expensive-to-replace hard parts. Not a bad sense of protection for just $250*!*

RESOURCE GUIDE

905 Racing
Engine cages, scrape bars
(619) 210-4777
racing905.com

Sharkskinz
Street replacement bodywork
(772) 388-9621
sharkskinz.com

Stuntlife.com
Links to freestyle parts
stuntlife.com

Lockhart Phillips
Crash bungs, bar ends, swingarm protectors
(800) 221-7291
lockhartphillipsusa.com

Making the most of his engine cage, Blake gets seriously horizontal!

INDEX

Other titles of interest:

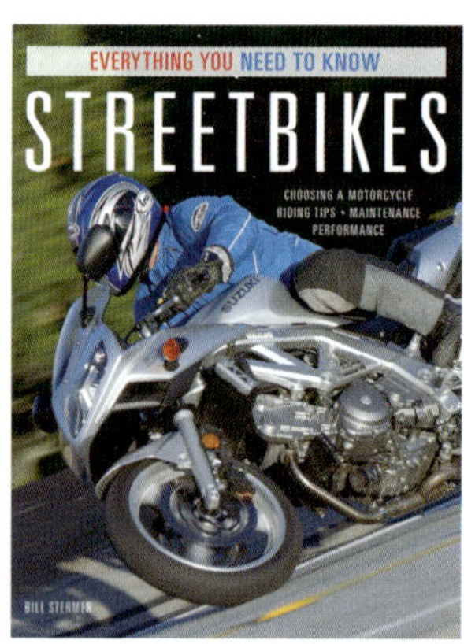

Streetbikes: Everything You Need to Know
0-7603-2362-3, 140295

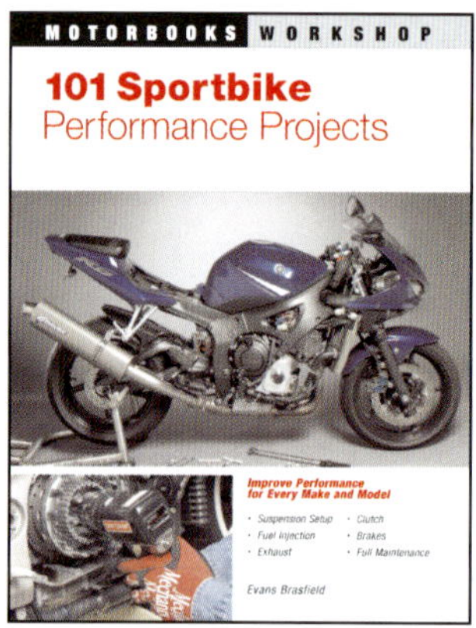

101 Sportbike Performance Projects
0-7603-1331-8, 135742

Sportbike Performance Handbook
0-7603-0229-4, 125118

Streetbike Extreme
0-7603-1299-0, 134895

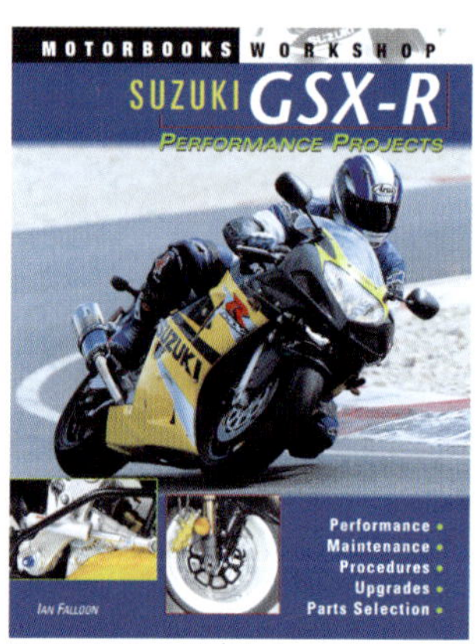

Suzuki GSX-R Performance Projects
0-7603-1546-9, 135884

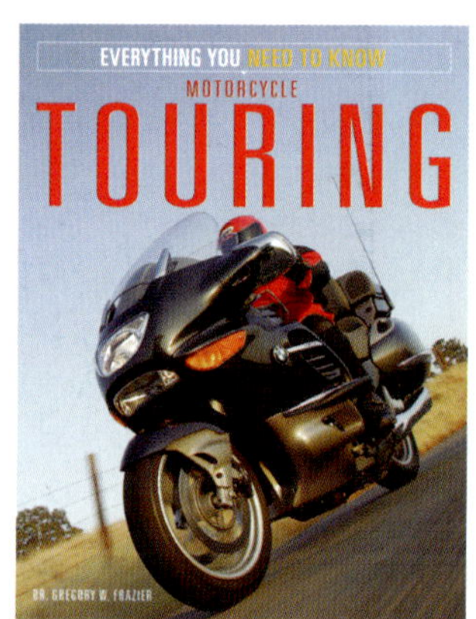

Motorcycle Touring: Everything You Need to Know
0-7603-2035-7, 138641

Techno Chop
0-7603-2116-7, 139362

How to Paint Your Motorcycle
0-7603-2078-0, 139431

How to Custom Paint Your Motorcycle
0-7603-2033-0, 138639